The
Human
Dimension
IN INTERNATIONAL
RELATIONS

The
Human
Dimension
IN INTERNATIONAL
RELATIONS

OTTO KLINEBERG
University of Paris

Holt, Rinehart and Winston
NEW YORK · CHICAGO · SAN FRANCISCO · TORONTO · LONDON

January, 1966

Printed in the United States of America

For
Rosemary, John, and Stephen

PREFACE

As this book goes to press, I face my potential readers with a mixture of confidence and concern. The confidence comes from a genuine belief in the contribution which the science of psychology can make to international relations, and from my conviction that I have brought together a wider range of relevant psychological material than can be found in any other single volume with which I am familiar. The concern takes the form of what French psychiatrists have called the *sentiment d'incomplétude,* the feeling that significant issues have been treated in too summary a fashion, that so much of importance has been left out. Almost every day brings to my desk new references that should be included and fresh research findings that should be presented and analyzed. Since reading the proofs of this book, for instance, I have received *The Journal of Social Issues* for July 1963, devoted to "Impacts of Studying Abroad," and the *Revue de Psychologie des Peuples* (No. 3, 1963) with an article on *négritude,* which I should have liked to include in Chapter 3. The field is alive and active, and no coverage could possibly be complete.

The interested student can, however, if he wishes, keep up with the relevant research by consulting the two journals mentioned in the preceding paragraph, as well as the *Journal of Conflict Resolution* and *Race* (published by the Institute of Race Relations in London). He can find in Elise Boulding's *International Newsletter on Peace Research,* Vol. I, No. I, 1963, a list of the Peace Research Centers in the world with an indication of the nature of the activities of each. From the Canadian Peace Research Institute in Toronto he can obtain a *Bibliography on War and Peace* compiled by Dr. Hanna Newcombe in August 1963; presumably this will be kept up to date. Both of these contain many items of psychological interest. Other valuable periodicals in this field include the *International Social Science Journal,* published by UNESCO in Paris, and *Information,* published by the International Social Science Council, also in Paris. A list of recent books which I would recommend for further reading follows the references at the end of this volume. Many of these have not been written by psychologists, but they all have psychological implications. They should really have been included in the discussion.

I referred above to the "interested student." It is my hope that this book may be used in colleges and universities, perhaps as a supplement to courses in social psychology and in international relations, possibly in other social sciences as well. I have tried, however, to write as clearly and simply as possible, with a minimum of undefined technical terms, so that the book might also be read by the interested layman who is beyond or outside the academic environment. It is not easy to write for two distinct kinds of reader, and I can only hope that I have been reasonably successful.

Portions of this book have already appeared in print, but have been modified to fit the present framework. I am grateful for the opportunity to use again material I wrote for *The Journal of Social Psychology*, *The International Social Science Bulletin* (UNESCO), *The Journal of Social Issues*, *Education*, *Mens en Maatschappij*, *Revista de la Universidad de Madrid*, *Rivista di Sociologia*, the *Festschrift* for Gardner Murphy, *Intergroup Relations and Leadership* (edited by M. Sherif), and the Encyclopaedia Britannica. In addition, I used a few paragraphs from an article which I wrote together with Richard Christie, published in summary form in *The Selection of Personnel for International Service* (edited by M. Torre); I am sure Christie will forgive me if some of the sentences I used here were written by him rather than by me!

This book owes much to many people; to the scholars whom I have quoted or whose work I have discussed; to my students at Columbia and the University of Paris on whom I tried out these ideas; to those at universities and other organizations in Europe as well as in the United States, who invited me to lecture, thus enabling me to clarify my own views in the process. My special thanks go to Gardner and Lois Murphy, who read an earlier draft of this book and gave me many suggestions for its improvement; to Eugene Jacobson, whose critical comments were very helpful; and to Marisa Zavalloni, who contributed so much of her spare time and energy to tracking down references, bringing new bibliography to my attention, and summarizing the content of books and journal articles.

My wife has literally or figuratively looked over my shoulder at almost every word I have written, challenging every phrase that was obscure and every comma that was out of place. Whatever style or clarity the book possesses owes a great deal to her intelligent criticism. I cannot adequately express my gratitude to her.

I am dedicating this book to my children, and through them to their children and to the children of all of us, in the hope that they will live in a world at peace.

O.K.

Paris
December 1963

CONTENTS

The
Human
Dimension
IN INTERNATIONAL
RELATIONS

The Minds of Men

*I have seen the outward appearance of the
city, but I have observed the manners of
men too little.*

Plautus

This book is a psychologist's approach to problems in the
field of international relations. It has been written in the conviction that psychology is rich enough and ripe enough to make
a contribution. We are reminded almost daily that our world is
in danger of destruction; we are not reminded often enough that
whether or not that danger is to be averted depends on the decisions of human beings, and that as a consequence an understanding of the factors influencing such decisions is absolutely
imperative. As Dr. Brock Chisholm, former Director General
of the World Health Organization, has expressed it: "We have
been slow to recognize that we are the first generation that holds
the veto power over the continuation of humanity." We have
also been slow to recognize that now for the first time we have
enough knowledge about human beings to help reduce the likelihood that such a veto power will be exercised.

The word "help" has been used advisedly. There are no easy solutions to problems as complicated as those with which humanity is faced, no panaceas, no healing miracles. There is, however, a body of scientific material, much of it already known to psychologists and other social scientists, most of it unfamiliar and relatively inaccessible to those outside these academic disciplines. If this material were more widely known and more generally accepted, it would contribute to an improvement in international relations now and in the future. In any case, the challenge to students of human behavior to apply their accumulated knowledge to the improvement of the international climate is one that cannot be ignored; the pages that follow represent the response of one psychologist to that challenge.

Although the problem of war and peace is central to the writer's concerns, he has interpreted the area of international relations broadly enough to include a number of marginal issues. The choice of the proper person to head an overseas mission, or the study of national characteristics, will have little direct or immediate bearing on whether or not a nuclear war will occur in the near future. The criteria for inclusion of any particular topic have been, first, that it be relevant to the relations between nations, and second, that psychology and the neighboring social sciences have a contribution to make in connection with it.

Such contributions can be envisaged under four major headings, with the understanding that the lines of demarcation are by no means complete or definite. There is, to begin with, the presentation of certain *factual data,* collected over many years through careful social science research, that have important practical implications for international relations. These are found in Chapters 2 to 7, and deal with the nature of aggressiveness, the international implications of relations among ethnic groups, the role of national stereotypes, the development of nationalistic attitudes, the influence of the leader, and the introduction of technical change into developing countries. The next two chapters (8 and 9) refer to *principles* of explanation that are psychological in nature and that are based on the one hand on psychoanalytic theory, and on the other, on the social psychology of perception. Chapters 10 to 12 inclusive refer to *techniques* that can be applied for the purpose of studying public opinion, evaluating the effectiveness of international programs, and selecting personnel for overseas service. These are followed by two chapters (13 and 14) in which recent research is examined for its implications for the understanding of national characteristics and for the decision-making process. In spite of the rather wide range of topics that have been included, it is clear that this little book by no means covers the whole field of international relations, not even all the areas that have psychological aspects.

The interest of psychologists and other social scientists in their potential contribution to international relations dates approximately from the end of World War II. As far back as 1944 a group of American psychologists prepared a statement on "Human Nature and the Peace." This was sent for endorsement to about 4000 psychologists throughout the country; 60 percent of them replied, and 99 percent of these approved and signed.

This statement, or manifesto, was issued at a time, shortly before the conclusion of the war, when major attention was directed toward improving the relationships between the victorious and the defeated nations. Some of its propositions are still pertinent. Psychologists are agreed, for example, that there is nothing in human nature that makes war inevitable, and they remind us also of the role of education and experience in overcoming racial, national, and group hatreds. The manifesto as a whole is important not only for its content, but as representing the first major recognition by psychologists that in addition to using their training and their skills to help their country win the war, they also had the responsibility to concern themselves with the problems of peace (Murphy, 1945).

Wider recognition of the importance of psychological factors both led to and resulted from the activities of UNESCO, the United Nations Educational, Scientific, and Cultural Organization. The preamble to the constitution of this organization contains the well-known words, "Since wars begin in the minds of men, it is in the minds of men that the defences of peace must be constructed." In addition, at the second session of the UNESCO General Conference held in Mexico City in 1947, it was decided to set up a project on "Tensions Affecting International Understanding" that, though oriented to all the social sciences, had a number of specifically psychological implications regarding sources of conflict between nations. These were especially marked in the proposed enquiries into (a) "the distinctive character of the various national cultures, ideals and legal systems" on the theory that more knowledge would lead to better relations (see below, Chapter 13); into (b) "the ideas which the people of one nation hold concerning their own and other nations" so that the effect of stereotypes might be reduced (Chapter 4); into (c) "modern methods . . . for changing mental attitudes" (Chapter 5); into (d) "the influences which make for international understanding or for aggressive nationalism" (Chapters 8, 9, and 14). They also entered into (e) the study of "population problems affecting international understanding, including the cultural assimilation of immigrants" (Chapter 3); and (f) "the influence of modern technology upon the attitudes and mutual relationships of peoples" (Chapter 7). The investigations stimulated directly or indirectly by the Tensions Project have made significant contributions to which reference will be made later; although the project as such no longer exists as a separate entity, many of its goals have been incorporated into the Division of Applied Social Sciences where they are being further developed.

Another landmark is represented by the publication in 1948 of a small brochure entitled "Mental Health and World Citizenship" under the auspices of the then newly formed World Federation for Mental Health. This statement, on which psychologists worked together with colleagues in psychiatry, anthropology, sociology, and other social sciences, summarized what was then known about the implications of the mental health disciplines for international understanding, stressing the conclusion that a major goal of mental health was to enable people to live together in One World. (A second statement, oriented toward more recent developments, was published in 1961 under the title "Mental Health in International Perspective.")

In the last decade, spurred by the rise in international tension, and concerned about making a contribution no matter how modest toward reducing the threat of nuclear war, psychologists and others who deal with human relations have increased their efforts to understand international conflict and to improve international relations.

The American Psychological Association and the Society for the Psychological Study of Social Issues both have active committees dealing with the potential contributions of psychologists to international affairs. The Swiss Society of Psychologists has called upon psychologists everywhere to direct their energies and their skills toward improving the relations between the peoples of the world; a similar appeal has been made by the International Association of Applied Psychology. Many local groups of psychologists have been formed to further the same goals. Neighboring disciplines such as psychiatry and anthropology have proceeded along comparable lines.

Physicists and engineers were perhaps quicker to recognize their responsibility in this area, their pride in the scientific achievement of releasing nuclear energy tempered by their fears as to how this energy would be used. The responsibility of psychologists and their colleagues, however, is at least as great. Human beings will determine whether or not to press the fateful button. Whose business is it, if not that of the psychologists and their colleagues in the other social sciences, to give us some understanding of human beings and of aspects of their behavior that lead to disturbed relationships and mutual threats of destruction?

Such understanding is by no means final or complete, and there are many occasions in this text when the writer has to point to areas in which more research is needed. There remains, however, a substantial body of psychological material relevant to international relations, on which one can rely with considerable confidence, based on the results of observation, clinical experience, and even laboratory experiments. It has seemed worthwhile at this particular crisis in our history to bring this material together, to try to organize it into a relatively coherent whole, to give a summary account of the facts, the insights, and the available techniques that represent the potential contribution of the psychologist. The attempt has been made to remain as close as possible to what has been demonstrated with scientific objectivity, but one cannot avoid the occasional intrusion of one's own judgment and value systems, and mistakes are not always avoidable.

The late S. F. Nadel (1951), referring to the case of anthropologists who are asked for advice concerning technological change and related problems, states that "the blunders of the anthropologists will be 'better' blunders" than those made by the layman. Perhaps the same modest claim can be made for the psychologist.

One claim that is not being made, however, is that the psychologist has all the answers. The solution of problems in the field of international relations requires the insights and the competence of political scientists, economists, historians, demographers, and many others. Psychological knowledge can be no substitute for theirs, but it can complement and supplement what they have to say. We have a right to ask that it, too, receive adequate consideration. We can go one step further and insist that since none of the other approaches has solved the problem of peace, ours at least deserves a hearing.

The UNESCO statement that wars begin in the minds of men has formed the basis of a continuing controversy. For some it has been an inspiration to work for international understanding through the application of psychological science; others have regarded it as absurd and meaningless. Those who have taken the negative view have usually argued that "the minds of men" are not the cause but the consequence of political events, that men are swayed by economic, demographic, and ideological forces beyond their control. It is impossible, however, to make this separation between the objective and the subjective. The so-called impersonal factors work in and through human beings; they are altered as the result of human relations.

An example may help to make this point clear. Campbell (1952) analyzed the responses of a sample of Americans to questions concerning their attitudes toward minority groups, particularly Jews. He found no consistent relation between the amount of anti-Semitism and an economic "fact" such as level of income; no clear tendency for those who were in superior economic positions to show less or more prejudice. When the respondents were classified, however, in terms of their degree of satisfaction or dissatisfaction with their economic position, a clear relationship emerged. "Those persons classified as dissatisfied with their own economic situation expressed hostility toward Jews more frequently than those who were economically satisfied." It was the economic fact as interpreted psychologically, the "psychoeconomic" fact, which was of crucial importance. Many other instances could be cited to indicate that there is a psychological component even in the so-called impersonal and objective factors that allegedly determine the shape of the world. The minds of men *are* important, and this book is directed toward demonstrating the fact and illustrating the range and influence of the human factor in international relations.

We turn now to some of the relevant psychological data that should have an educational impact if they were more widely disseminated and understood. The first question that will be raised refers to the position of psychologists regarding the nature of aggressiveness in man. If human nature makes war inevitable, there would be hardly any point in going on with the rest of this book. Is native aggressiveness the cause of war?

2

Why War?

*War is much too serious a matter to be left
to military men.*

Talleyrand. Quoted by Briand to
Lloyd George during World War I.

A number of years ago an American anthropologist, George
Dorsey (1925), wrote a book with the intriguing title *Why We
Behave Like Human Beings*. The search for the springs of human
action, the motivating forces by which we are impelled, has been
a continuing concern throughout the history of philosophy and
social science. The question involved lies at the very root of the
understanding of human nature. Sometimes action is explained
on the basis of a single overriding principle such as the pursuit
of pleasure and the avoidance of pain; sometimes a list is presented, varying in length and content, of allegedly inborn, universal springs of action, usually termed "instincts."

Among these, the one that has the most obvious implications
for our topic, the one that constitutes in the minds of many the
greatest stumbling block to constructive and cooperative international relations, is the so-called instinct of pugnacity, hostility,

or (most commonly) aggression. From this the consequence is frequently drawn that war is a fundamental characteristic of human nature. If, as there is good reason to believe (Chapter 9), the expectation of war may in itself be a cause of war, the conviction that it is inevitable may have important practical consequences.

This conviction is evidently widely held. A National Opinion Research Center poll in 1947 found that over 70 percent of Americans believed that war is inevitable. In a survey of the attitudes of school teachers and factory workers in France and the United States in 1961, the respondents were specifically asked whether this was so because of "human nature"; a majority answered in the affirmative (Dubourg, 1962).

To return to the question of an aggressive instinct, the first point that must be made is that the very concept of instinct has fallen into disrepute among almost all psychologists, with the one major exception of the psychoanalysts. Psychologists do not deny the existence or importance of the biological component in human behavior, but they see that component as so intimately integrated and interconnected with social factors as to justify describing the whole complex as *biosocial* in character. (See, for example, Gardner Murphy, *Personality: A Biosocial Approach,* 1947.) This does not mean a mere addition of so much social to so much biological; there is rather a constant and continuing interpenetration that justifies us in saying, paradoxical though this may sound, that all our actions are due 100 percent to heredity and 100 percent to the (social) environment. Even among animals it has been demonstrated that what has in the past been called "instinctive" depends for its functioning on the maintenance of a particular environment. Thus it is usually said that a baby duckling will *instinctively* follow its mother, but if at an early stage in its development a human being makes appropriate sounds in its presence, what has been called "imprinting" will occur: the duckling will follow that person and may later do so *in preference* to following its own mother (Lorenz, 1952).

When we turn to allegedly instinctive behavior in man, and more particularly to aggressive behavior, we are immediately struck by the great variations found between individuals and between groups. Conflicts certainly arise everywhere; one may even regard them as inevitable, but there is nothing inevitable about the way in which they are expressed, or in the reactions they elicit. Anthropologists have supplied us with ample evidence on this point; the following examples illustrate the range of solutions in different cultural groups when a conflict arises between two individuals.

When the Mrus of India had a difference of opinion they called in an exorcist who found out from the spirits how the matter should be decided. A grievance between two Santa Marta Indians in Colombia was settled by going to a rock or large tree, each disputant carrying a stick. They would then strike violently at the tree or rock, at the same time uttering a multitude of insulting words, until one of them cracked or broke his stick; he was regarded as the victor, and the dispute was settled. Among the Crow Indians personal brawls were regarded with contempt and occurred very rarely, and the same is reported for several of the groups visited by Livingstone in Africa.

Among the Indians of British Columbia and the northwest coast of the United States, disputes were usually settled through the institution known as the potlatch, in which the means of winning an argument consisted of giving away or destroying as large an amount of property as possible. In a quarrel, one man might give a potlatch to show that he was really superior, and his opponent would be regarded as the loser until he could restore his prestige by giving a bigger potlatch himself. A chief from one of those tribes (the Kwakiutl) once said: "The white man fights with his hands, but we fight with property." The Eskimo usually settled an argument through a public duel or contest in which the contestants appeared before the little village community and sang satirical and abusive songs about each other, rattling all possible skeletons in the enemy's cupboard, so that he would be humbled and ridiculed in the eyes of the judges. The victory went to the one who sang the more effective song. It seems clear that whether an individual fights with satire or with property or with his fists will be decided by the traditions and customs of his group.

In a culture as complex as our own, we also find a wide range of "aggressive" behaviors, without having to go so far afield as Africa or aboriginal British Columbia. We do fight with our fists, occasionally, and even with deadlier weapons; we also fight with words, either formally in a court of law, or informally over the back fence; we fight with property too, as when bigger parties are given to determine who is really the social leader of a community. Aggression may be expressed by working hard on a job in order to beat a rival; or by keeping silent when one is asked to speak up in another's behalf; or through a social snub; or by committing suicide on the doorstep of the girl by whom one has been rejected.

As has already been indicated, orthodox psychoanalysts usually continue to speak of instincts, including the instinct of aggression (Freud's Thanatos, the death instinct); this would indicate that they regard it as inevitable and universal *in some form*. These last three words are crucial. They indicate that even for the strict Freudian there is nothing inevitable about any specific aggressive act, since the "instinct" can be expressed through the potlatch or the Eskimo linguistic duel, and not necessarily through physical attack on the enemy. If one adds to this the concept of sublimation, which in Freudian theory performs the function of redirecting the energy generated by aggression into socially approved channels (like painting a picture or climbing a high mountain), the inevitability of physical hostility is greatly reduced.

The question of the universality of aggression is further complicated by considerable difference in the definition of the term itself. One writer (Lauretta Bender, 1948), for example, refers to the original meaning of aggression as a tendency to go forward or approach. This is regarded as instinctive, whereas the inborn or instinctive nature of *hostility* has never been demonstrated. Another (F. H. Allen, 1948) describes it as the will to assert and to test our capacity to deal with external forces, and it is this, rather than hostility, that is a fundamental characteristic of all living beings. It seems probable that agreement could be reached on the universality of such a characteristic, but this would be irrelevant for present purposes, since it is hostility or destructive aggression that is crucial to international relations, and, in what follows, the term "aggression" will continue to be used with this negative connotation.

Allied to the psychoanalytic approach is the theory that aggression is due to frustration, and that frustration always leads to aggression (Dollard *et al.*, 1939). If this theory were sound, it would mean that aggression is a reactive, rather than a primary, phenomenon; that is to say, it would occur *only* as a reaction to some form of frustration or failure on the part of the individual to reach a desired goal. This distinction may seem trivial for practical purposes, since the process of socialization, through which the child gradually becomes adapted to the values and regulations of his group, must inevitably involve frustration, and as an outcome, aggression. It may still be true, however— and this would have far-reaching practical consequences—that the greater the frustration, the greater, correspondingly, will be the aggression.

As we shall see, there is some truth in this important proposition, but it requires modification in several respects. In the first place, people differ in what has been termed "frustration tolerance"; that is, the capacity to accept frustration without any obvious or marked reaction. Secondly, when they do react, they differ in the extent to which they show aggression and the direction in which it is expressed. They may work harder in order to reach their goal; they may discover new paths, new methods; they may become resigned or apathetic or resort to the "sour grapes" mechanism—the goal was not worth reaching in the first place; they may regress to a form of behavior that was appropriate earlier; they may find new, substitute goals. In other words they *may* show aggression, but not necessarily, and when they do, it may take many different forms and produce many different results. Thirdly, but related to the above, people may *learn* to be either aggressive or nonaggressive in the face of a frustrating situation. In terms of learning theory, their aggression may be reinforced if it brings success or satisfaction, or it may be extinguished —or nearly so—if it goes unrewarded. These various limitations support the conclusion that whether reactive or primary, aggression expresses itself in so many ways, to such different degrees, and under such varying conditions, that no specific form of hostile behavior can be safely predicted.

This means that war cannot be ascribed to an alleged aggressive instinct. As has already been indicated, an overwhelming number of psychologists agreed that "war is not born in man." The capacity for aggressive behavior may be a necessary antecedent to war, but it is clearly not the sole or effective cause. This conclusion is strengthened by anthropological evidence which indicates the many different motives which may be involved (Klineberg, 1935).

In the case of many wars among the so-called primitive peoples, as in complex civilizations, material interests undoubtedly played a prominent part. On Chatham Island fights were usually for the possession of the flesh of whales and other sea animals. In parts of South Africa, wars took place over cattle, and it is said that several tribes refused to keep livestock so as not to tempt their enemies. War among the Cheyenne Indians was rare until the white man introduced horses, which furnished a new and powerful motive for war because something could then be gained by it. To the extent that wars are fought for national gain, it would be salutary to keep in mind that in a nuclear war both sides must inevitably lose.

Wars have occurred also for religious reasons; the Aztecs of Mexico carried on constant warfare with the Tlaxcalans, evidently for the sole purpose of obtaining human sacrifices regarded as necessary to renew the strength of their gods. Among many peoples, also, raids on neighboring groups for the possession of their women occurred with some frequency. The quest for glory was evidently the predominant motive for the Plains Indians, who had special rules for "counting coup" as evidence of their bravery, and among whom killing an enemy was subordinate to the desire for prestige. Many other examples could be given (Quincy Wright, *The Causes of War*, 1935).

It has been argued that such factors operate in relatively simple, uncomplicated social systems, and that their relevance for modern warfare must therefore be questioned. This is the position taken, for example, by Raymond Aron (1962). Granting that the situations are indeed very different, our present concern is with the relationship between war and an allegedly innate aggressiveness, and in this context any examples from any society may be used to illustrate the fact that many different motives may be involved. Besides, it is not so far back in our own history that the Crusades were undertaken for the glory of Christianity, and that Moslems fought to convert others to their faith. As far as material gain is concerned, that is as clearly a motive for complex societies as it is for the simpler ones. The point that is being made is that there are many causes of war, not just a direct or even indirect expression of aggressive impulses.

This latter theory has had its proponents, however. One psychoanalyst (Pryns Hopkins, *The Psychology of Social Movements,* 1938) has argued that the anger and resentment of the child against his father develop a latent aggressiveness that seeks an outlet, and finds it in the "enemy," accepted by the whole community as a legitimate object of hostility. The frustration-aggression theory, to which reference was made above, assumes that, when people are frustrated, they will be more likely to resort to war as a means of expressing their aggression. Two British writers (Durbin and Bowlby, *Personal Aggressiveness and War,* 1939) argue similarly that frustrations in early childhood create adults who, often unconsciously, want war; consequently the best way to prevent war is to reduce such early frustrations, and thereby remove the need to find an "enemy" upon whom to exercise one's latent hostility. Variations on this theme occur with some frequency in the writings of psychoanalysts or of those influenced by psychoanalytic theory (see Strachey, *The Unconscious Motives of War,* 1956).

This explanation of war strikes the present writer as definitely unsatisfactory and inadequate. In the first place, every modern nation in time of war has had to resort to some form of draft or conscription to satisfy the manpower needs of its armed forces. If all of us were eagerly awaiting a chance to express a latent aggression stored up for years, would coercion be required to build up an army? Would we not all rush to enlist instead of, in most cases, awaiting the summons?

There are other questions, perhaps less rhetorical, that require an answer. Is there any indication that people who start wars are more frustrated than those who do their best to stay out of them? Are pacifists less frustrated than those ready to go to war? Have the Swedes and the Swiss, who have managed to stay out of wars for some time, had a less frustrating childhood than the Germans or the Japanese? The Swedes, for one, had many wars during a considerable period of their history, and then they changed. Is there any evidence that this was accompanied by a corresponding improvement in the relations between parents and children?

The writer is not suggesting that the experience of individuals, including parent-child relations and early and later frustrations and setbacks, play no part in shaping attitudes toward war. He is insisting, rather, that this approach does not tell the whole story, and that many other factors must be taken into account. Personal aggressiveness, whether primary or reactive, is definitely not an adequate explanation of war.

Two additional considerations are relevant in this connection. The first is that only a tiny fraction of those engaged in modern warfare are given any direct opportunity to show whatever aggressiveness, latent or overt, they may possess. The number of men engaged in office work, supply and transport, communication, medical care, construction of roads and airstrips, maintenance and repair of machinery, and so on, is far in excess of those who ever see the enemy face to face. Personal aggressiveness, except of a very indirect character, has little chance for expression. It has been estimated that in World War II, for every man actively engaged in combat, more than ten were involved in activity behind the lines. If there should ever be a World War III, most of the chances to express "aggression" would be allocated to machines.

The second point that needs to be made is that, although man has potentialities for destructive aggression, he also has tendencies toward affiliation and cooperation. Although we are not in a position to decide which of these two human capacities is stronger or more widespread, there is some evidence to indicate that the altruistic motive exerts at least as much influence as its opposite. Among animals, for example, as one ascends the phylogenetic scale, genuinely altruistic behavior increases in frequency, and it is well-developed in the chimpanzee (Hebb and Thompson, 1954). As far as human beings are concerned, striking results were obtained in a study during World War II of men in combat; that is, in a situation giving the maximum opportunity for the expression of attitudes of hostility (Stouffer *et al.,* 1949). These men were asked, "When the going was tough, how much were you helped by thoughts of hatred for the enemy?" About *one third* said such thoughts "helped a lot." When they were asked, however, "How much did it help you to think that you couldn't let the other men down?" about *two thirds* gave this answer. Allport (1960) comments that "the affiliative motive, even under extreme stress, seems to hold twice as many men to their task as does the motive of hate." The psychiatrist Jerome Frank (1960), in discussing this same issue, writes: "The only reasonable conclusion concerning man's innate endowment is that he has both altruistic and self-aggrandizing trends, and that both are very strong." One need only add that man is sufficiently malleable, so that either of these trends may be magnified or reduced by the particular learning experiences to which he is subjected. Man's *capacity* for aggressive behavior does not necessarily lead to war.

A variant of the view that human aggressiveness causes wars is represented by the theory that in animals as well as in man, a fundamental impulse is to maintain "territoriality." Ardrey (1961) argues that fights arise when one's territory is attacked or threatened, and that throughout the animal kingdom this is what causes individual and group conflict. As has already been pointed out, however, there are many different causes of conflict, and many ways of resolving it, and the exclusive emphasis on one motive and one outcome hardly carries conviction.

To repeat, there is nothing in human nature that makes war inevitable. This conclusion is strengthened by the undeniable fact that warfare is by no means a universal phenomenon. Not only have all, or nearly all, peoples enjoyed long periods of peace, but there are some among whom war, as far as we know, never occurred. After surveying the cultural characteristics of a large number of groups, Hobhouse and his associates (1915) concluded that there were at least ten that apparently had never gone to war. The Arctic explorer Nansen (1893) quotes a letter written by an Eskimo in 1756 that is illuminating in this connection. The Eskimo, after having received an explanation of war in economic terms, apostrophizes his own country: "How well it is that you are covered with ice and snow! Your unfruitfulness makes us happy and saves us from molestation." He then expresses surprise that Europeans had not learned better ways among the Eskimo, and—the crowning touch—proposes to send medicine men as missionaries to the whites to teach them the Eskimo way of life!

War, then, is not inevitable, but this is cold comfort to a world in imminent danger of destruction should another great war occur. There is therefore no question more crucial than the one that heads this chapter, *Why War?* The writer cannot hope to provide a fully satisfactory answer, but in the pages that follow he has attempted an analysis of some of the psychological factors that seem to him at least in part responsible. With so much at stake, no possible road to understanding should be neglected. If war is too serious a matter to be left to military men, surely peace is too serious a matter to be left entirely to politicians.

In the next chapter one of these psychological factors is discussed; namely, the belief in the inherent superiority of certain racial and ethnic groups over others, with the frequent corollary that the "superior" group has the right to conquer, exploit, and even destroy those considered "inferior." Man is often governed by myths, and among these none is more important or more devastating in its consequences than the myth of race.

3

The Myth of Race

*Of all the vulgar modes of escaping from
the consideration of the effect of social
and moral influence upon the human mind,
the most vulgar is that of attributing the
diversities of conduct and character to
inherent natural differences.*

J. S. Mill, *Principles of Political
Economy,* 1848.

It would be very difficult to overestimate the tremendous part
played by ideas of race, of racial identity, and of alleged inborn
racial differences in mentality, in shaping the relations between
the peoples and nations of the world. These ideas have contributed
to the deaths of millions of people, paved the way for war, created
wounds that will not heal, produced enmities that—at least for
a long time to come—will not die. Although it may be difficult
to predict just what course these ideas will follow in the future,
there is not much doubt about what they have done to the world
in the fairly recent past.

A striking feature of these ideas is the fact that they have
usually been based on a false conception of the meaning of race
and on erroneous assumptions regarding its implications. Jacques
Barzun (1937), for example, entitles his book on this subject,
Race: a Study in Modern Superstition. Ashley Montagu (1945)

speaks of *Man's Most Dangerous Myth: The Fallacy of Race.*
Gunnar Myrdal (1944) in his *An American Dilemma* expresses
the opinion that in no other field is there so wide a gap between
popular impressions and the conclusions reached by biological
and social scientists. Race in many of its aspects exists only "in
the minds of men."

This has not prevented people and governments from taking
race very seriously indeed. Although there is neither an Aryan
nor a Jewish "race" in any accepted scientific meaning of the
term, Hitler and the Nazis made this alleged distinction one of the
cornerstones of their policy, with results that are only too well
known. There were of course inner contradictions in the racist
approach; the fact that so many Germans did not look like
Nordics and so many Jews did, the alliance with the Japanese who
had consequently to be exempted from the racial restrictions of
the Third Reich, the difficulty of giving any clear meaning to the
concepts of German "blood" or "soul" so that facts had to be replaced by mysticism. In spite of these and other deficiencies,
racism was used as a technique to unify the Germans by identifying the "enemy," to give the people a strong sense of ego-enhance-
ment and self-confidence, to justify economic exploitation and
slave labor, to obtain support for the war, and to convince the
Germans that they could never be defeated. Racism thus functioned as one of the most effective techniques of Nazi propaganda
for acquiring and maintaining power over the German people.
It was important in precipitating World War II and responsible
for its special character.

Although colonialism cannot be compared with Nazism in terms
of the violence and extent of the human destruction it involved,
it also found in racism a helpful rationalization for conquest and
expansion. When the Spaniards first came to America, several of
their apologists, particularly Quevedo and Sepulveda, supplied
them with the proper excuses for taking the land away from the
Indians and for treating them with complete lack of consideration.
They developed the theory that the Indians had an entirely different origin from that of the Spaniards, that they were not human
in the same sense, and that there was therefore no need to accord
them the same treatment as to one's fellow human beings. Later,

the familiar refrain of the "white man's burden," which was mainly of British manufacture and found its literary expression in the writings of Carlyle, Froude, Kingsley, and most clearly in those of Kipling, made of imperialism a noble activity destined to bring civilization to the benighted members of other "races." What the British stood to gain as a result was never mentioned. Similarly, the French justified the maintenance of their colonial empire on the basis of their *mission civilisatrice,* their duty to bring civilization to the backward peoples of the world.

In all of these colonizing empires there were undoubtedly many individuals honestly convinced of the nobility of their motives and their enterprise; at the same time, the feelings of racial superiority accompanying colonialism played an important part in developing resentments among the colonized that have often survived even the recent trend toward emancipation and independence.

The most extreme contemporary example of racism is found in South Africa, which has withdrawn from the British Commonwealth as a direct consequence of the practice and philosophy of *apartheid.* Its position in the United Nations and the specialized agencies of the United Nations has become exceedingly precarious, its relations with India and with the new African states have been strained to the breaking point, the resentment that has developed among Africans in general threatens the peace of the whole continent.

As far as the United States is concerned, colonialism as such has played a relatively minor role in our history, but since our alliances have usually been with nations identified with the colonizing process, we have frequently been put in the same category. In addition, our own treatment of minorities has given support to those who have placed us in the camp of the racists and has certainly affected our relations with many other nations. The whole history of our immigration laws, especially the various Oriental Exclusion Acts, undoubtedly contributed to the deterioration of our relations with Japan and must bear some of the responsibility for Pearl Harbor. As Roger Baldwin has expressed it (1949), "Of all major countries in the world the United States has by law most deliberately insulted all Asiatic peoples by declaring them unfit for immigration and for citizenship." During a period of twenty years, he adds, from 1924 to 1945, "we served notice on over half of mankind that they were not racially qualified to associate with us" (p. 83). Further, "It was this very Exclusion Act which after 1924 so largely contributed to the defeat of the liberals in Japanese politics as to make possible the rise of the militarists" (p. 86). In Baldwin's judgment, this did more than any other factor to break the bonds of friendship with the American people and set Japan on the road to war with America.

The treatment of the Negro in the United States has also had very definite international repercussions. With regard to our relations with Latin America, Berle has written (1949),

> to say that racial discrimination damages the Good Neighbor policy is a masterpiece of understatement. . . . the habit of race discrimination practiced in considerable parts of the United States is the greatest single danger to the foreign relations of the United States. . . . (pp. 91–92)

Our inability to arrive at a complete solution of this problem has placed us at a considerable disadvantage in the competition with the U.S.S.R. to gain the friendship and cooperation of many of the new nations. The fact that the Soviet Union has been guilty of its own variety of "colonialism" in relation to the Baltic States, Hungary, and other areas has not had the same impact because it has mainly involved Europeans, and has therefore not been interpreted in "racial" terms.

These are examples of the effect of our domestic policies on our relations with other countries. The reverse phenomenon also deserves attention; that is, the impact of the international situation on intergroup relations within the United States. For the country as a whole, there is good reason to believe that the Cold War and the desire on the part of the United States to face the darker-skinned peoples of the world with "clean hands," have heightened the country's awareness of the need to come to terms with the Negro problem. Statements by government officials are filled with references to this *because* of the international situation. Some northern newspaper accounts of the New Orleans resistance to desegregation have referred to the rioting women as "traitors to their country." Whether the international implications were in the minds of the Supreme Court judges who unanimously ruled against segregation in education is difficult to determine, but a good case could be made for the proposition that our international commitments have hastened the process of the more complete extension of civil rights to Negroes.

The term "racism in reverse" has been used for the phenomenon of antiwhite prejudice on the part of colored peoples. Its use suggests that racism is an invention of the whites, and it may be argued that it is a misnomer, since groups of all kinds have throughout history shown in varying degrees a dislike of the unlike. The fact remains that prejudice which takes a specifically "racial" form, that is, which becomes attached to differences in inherited physical characteristics, has been more frequently associated with the attitudes of whites who have occupied a position of dominance over darker-skinned subject peoples. It may therefore be appropriate to use the expression "racism in reverse" for recent developments in the opposite direction.

The phenomenon has taken many forms. The very existence of an Afro-Asian bloc is to some extent due to an antiwhite or at the very least a distinct-from-white orientation. The notion of *négritude* in the writings of intellectuals in Haiti, Martinique, and French-speaking Africa, usually has a cultural and literary orientation, a back-to-African-origins emphasis, but it also involves in many cases a belief in the superiority of black over white. Biesheuvel (1959), for example, speaks of *négritude* as a battle-cry in French West Africa, a means whereby those who are striving to rediscover their African identity are drawn together. This may supply the Africans with a meaningful new culture. At the same time, it is often associated with a conviction that the white world is dying and that the new vitality, the new life force, is to be found among the black peoples. A study of Senegalese elites by Mercier (1956) also shows that a revival of an interest in African culture may take the form of "a veritable mythology around the notion of 'Negrohood' and of a sort of 'counter-racism', the end-result of which is to shut the door on the outside world" (p. 441). The new African nationalism frequently shows racial overtones, and the reports of the rioting in the Congo, Angola, and elsewhere indicate that generalized antiwhite attitudes may play a significant role.

The theory of black superiority has developed into a cult among the so-called Black Muslims in the United States, the Rastafarians in Jamaica, and similar groups elsewhere. It is difficult to know with certainty how effective these movements have been or how widespread is their influence, but they are certainly causing concern to whites and Negroes alike. One occasionally hears a defense of "racism in reverse" on the ground that it is after all only a reaction to preceding white racism and that it supplies a feeling of dignity and self-esteem to people who for so long have been burdened with a sense of inferiority. The present writer can only express his own opinion that any philosophy that results in judging a people or an individual by the color of the skin, whether that skin be "white" or "black" or "brown" or "yellow," is inappropriate and unrealistic. White racism appears to be on the decline, slowly but unmistakably, and it would be tragic to see it revivified or supplemented or replaced by other forms of the same disease.

Throughout this presentation we have used the term "race" without defining it. A satisfactory definition is difficult to find. There is general agreement that it is correctly applied to a subdivision of mankind distinguished by the possession of common characteristics, usually physical in their nature, determined by genetic or hereditary factors. Popularly it has been confused with "nation," although it is obvious that every modern nation is a mixture of inherited physical types: there is no British or Italian or German race. As a matter of fact, there is more physical or racial similarity between northern Italians and southern Germans than between the latter and Germans living in Hanover or Prussia. Similarly there has been confusion between race and language; there is no Latin or Semitic or Aryan (Indo-European) race, since these languages are spoken by people of widely varying physical type. It follows that many of the phenomena usually included within the field of "race relations" have nothing to do with "race" as scientifically defined, but rather with "race" as popularly, and erroneously, understood.

Difficulties of application remain even when care is taken

to use "race" in the manner proposed by scientists. The geneticist Leslie Dunn (1951), for example, believes that the word may have a valid biological meaning if applied to a group of related intermarrying individuals differing from other groups in the relative commonness of certain hereditary traits. This leaves unresolved the question of how large the group should be, or which traits should be used for purposes of classification. Sergi, using head form as a criterion, proposes two races, the Eurasiatic or round-headed, and the Eurafrican or long-headed. Deniker, relying upon a combination of features including head form, skin color, and others, concludes that there are seventeen main races and twenty-nine subraces. If the criterion of head form is preferred, the blondest Scandinavian and the darkest Negro are united in the same category when both are long-headed. If the more usual category of skin color is used, differences in head form are ignored or at least relegated to the background. This means essentially that racial classification at the present stage of our knowledge is at least to some extent an arbitrary and subjective process. A group of experts called in by UNESCO expressed the view that three major human divisions should be recognized; namely, the Mongoloid, Negroid, and Caucasoid, and this is probably as satisfactory a classification as any now available, but it does not include all human groups, nor does it solve all the problems that have been raised. The reliance on blood properties, particularly the four blood types, A, B, AB, and O, has facilitated significant genetic research, but has not as yet produced a satisfactory racial classification.

In view of these complications, it has been suggested that the word "race" should not be applied to existing human populations, but should be replaced by the term "ethnic group," which may be characterized by a particular inherited physical type, or culture, or nationality, or any combination of these. In any case, the geneticists have made it clear that the inherited similarities among all the peoples of the world are much greater and far more common than the differences, and that the distinctions that have been drawn between the so-called races of mankind are relatively unimportant from the biological point of view.

In spite of the unscientific and contradictory character of the popular notion of race, the fact remains that it has played and continues to play a vital role in the relations between men. Accepting for purposes of argument the racial distinctions usually made, we must now turn to a crucial question: Is there any scientifically acceptable evidence of the innate superiority of any "race" over any other?

This issue has been approached from a number of different directions. It has been suggested, for example, that some groups are biologically more primitive, closer to our common animal origins. This position has been repudiated by scientists, who find no difference in the number of "primitive" traits in, for example, Negroes and whites (Kroeber, 1923).

A distinguished group of physical anthropologists and geneticists, meeting in UNESCO House in Paris in June 1951, issued the following statement:

> The differences in physical structure which distinguish one major group from another give no support to popular notions of any general "superiority" or "inferiority" which are sometimes implied in referring to these groups.

Another argument, and the one most frequently used, is based on the relative contributions of various groups to contemporary civilization, and the assumption that differences in this respect justify the conclusion that some "races" are inherently superior to others. This argument is much more complex, but the following considerations indicate the difficulties involved in the attempt to equate culture with "race." First, there is the question of finding a criterion universally applicable. Is a Benin sculpture superior or inferior to an Italian painting? Does it require more or less ability to follow a track through the Australian bush than to repair the carburetor of an automobile? Is it more intelligent to build a nuclear bomb than to live at peace with one's neighbors? Second, there is the undeniable fact that, whatever criteria we use, there is tremendous variation in the cultures of different subgroups within the same "race." The Incas of Peru and the "primitive" tribes of the Brazilian Mato Grosso are both American Indian; the complex civilization of classical China and the simple social structures of northern Siberia are the products of peoples similar in their Mongoloid physical characteristics. Third, there is the problem of time perspective; it is only quite recently, in the long history of man, that certain groups, particularly of European origin, have acquired a position of ascendancy. We tend to ignore the fact that in the past other "racial" groups had a life and culture that compared in complexity with our own (Herskovits, 1944). In this connection it is illuminating to remind ourselves that Aristotle in the fifth century b.c. was certain that the cold climate of northern Europe would result in a lack of intelligence among the peoples living there, so that they would be permanently unfitted for political organization and domination.

The psychologist's contribution to this issue lies in the development of a method of appraisal not dependent on purely subjective judgments. The psychological test permits us to present a series of problems to two groups of subjects, and the determination can then be made as to which group solves these problems more quickly or more effectively. If someone else doubts the results he may repeat the study, using the same or other subjects, and the same or other tests. This is all that would be necessary to settle the question of superior and inferior "races," if psychological tests were perfect instruments for the measurement of native or innate differences in ability. For a time they were accepted as such, at least by some psychologists and educators, as well as by many laymen. We now know that they are far from perfect. They still have important uses as measures of present capacity, but this capacity is clearly not due to innate intelligence alone.

The UNESCO "Statement on Race," formulated by social scientists in 1950, included the following judgment:

> It is now generally recognized that intelligence tests do not in themselves enable us to differentiate safely between what is due to innate capacity and what is the result of environmental influences, training and education. Wherever it has been possible to make allowances for differences in environmental opportunities, the tests have shown essential similarity in mental characters among all human groups.

(This should be interpreted to refer to all large groups of human beings, and not to individuals.)

Without entering into details concerning the relevant research, it may be worthwhile to note the striking change that has occurred in the thinking of many scientists who have concerned themselves with this problem. The reasons vary, but the fact is significant. As a first example, the late Howard W. Odum, formerly Professor of Sociology at the University of North Carolina, published in 1910 a volume on *Social and Mental Traits of the Negro,* in which he expressed the definite conviction that Negroes were inherently inferior to whites, and that they should be given the kind of education adapted to their poorer mental equipment. In 1936, Odum wrote an article on "The Errors of Sociology," published in Volume XV of the journal *Social Forces.* Among these errors Odum lists "the assumption that races are inherently different rather than group products of differentials due to the cumulative power of folk-regional and cultural environment."

In 1923 the late C. C. Brigham, Professor of Psychology at Princeton University, published *A Study of American Intelligence,* in which he reported his analysis of the results obtained through the application of intelligence tests to more than a million recruits in the American army in World War I. Since these recruits included many immigrants and sons of immigrants, as well as Negroes, Brigham compared the results obtained by various ethnic groups and found that whites were on the average superior to Negroes; among the whites, North Europeans (Nordics) were superior to Central Europeans (Alpines) who in turn were superior to South Europeans (Mediterraneans). The assumption was made that the tests measured differences in native intelligence. This study of Brigham's was widely read and frequently quoted. The suggestion has even been made that it was a factor in determining the quota system in United States immigration policy. Brigham himself changed his mind only a few years later about the meaning and significance of his analysis. As the result of a statistical study of the relationship between the various parts of the intelligence tests applied, he concluded that the method used was not scientifically sound. In an article on "Intelligence Tests of Immigrant Groups" published in the *Psychological Review* in 1930, he wrote: "As this method was used by the writer in his earlier analysis of the Army tests as applied to samples of the foreign-born in the draft, that study with its entire superstructure of racial differences collapses completely." Brigham points out also that language differences may have played a part, since many of the groups tested were bilingual, or spoke their own native language much better than they did English.

One final example of the change in point of view may be of interest. Florence L. Goodenough, Professor of Psychology at the University of Minnesota, published an article in 1926 in the *Journal of Experimental Psychology* on "Racial Differences in the Intelligence of School Children." She used her own "Draw-a-Man" test, in which achievement is measured in terms of how accurately a man is drawn, without regard to the esthetic qualities of the drawing. Since the test makes no use of language or "information," she believed it could be regarded as a test of native intelligence, independent of culture or previous experience. She reported that her groups differed in economic background, but she regarded this as irrelevant to her results. She wrote:

> It seems probable, upon the whole, that inferior environment is an effect at least as much as it is a cause of inferior ability. . . . The person of low intelligence tends to gravitate to those neighborhoods where economic requirement is minimal. . . . His children inherit his mental characteristics.

In other words, her conclusion was that there are racial differences in native ability, and that the results of the application of an intelligence test reveal the existence of such differences.

In a later publication (September, 1950), Professor Goodenough, writing with Dale B. Harris on "Studies in the Psychology of Children's Drawings" in the *Psychological Bulletin* reviews many of the investigations made with the "Draw-a-Man" test and concludes that there is a definite indication of the influence of culture and previous training on the results obtained. The test is not so "culture-free" as was formerly believed. Goodenough and Harris state in this article that they "would like to express the opinion that the search for a culture-free test, whether of intelligence, artistic ability, personal-social characteristics, or any other measurable trait is illusory, and that the naive assumption that the mere freedom from verbal requirements renders a test equally suitable for all groups is no longer tenable." In a footnote Goodenough states that her earlier study reporting differences among the children of immigrants to the United States "is certainly no exception to the rule. The writer hereby apologizes for it."

These honest and courageous admissions on the part of three distinguished scholars are mentioned here because they represent in clearest form the development that has taken place in this whole field of enquiry. The history of the mental testing of ethnic or racial groups may almost be described as a progressive disillusionment with tests as measures of native ability, and a gradually increasing realization of the many complex environmental factors that enter into the result.

The present consensus among experts who have studied this question as objectively and as scientifically as possible, is that there is no scientific proof of innate racial differences in intelligence; that the obtained differences in test results are best explained in terms of factors in the social and educational environment; that as the environmental opportunities of different racial or ethnic groups become more similar, the observed differences in test results also tend to disappear.

There are a few psychologists who support the position that there are indeed inborn psychological differences between racial groups (Shuey, 1958). They do so usually on the ground that even when such groups, that is, Negroes and whites, are "equated" for socioeconomic status or schooling, some difference in the intelligence quotient can still be demonstrated. This would be a very important point if the two groups concerned could really be "equated" for all the factors that play a part in determining the capacities measured by the intelligence tests. It is precisely this kind of "equating" that is not possible in those situations where one of the two groups is subjected to the effects of prejudice or discrimination. There will still be experiences and opportunities open to the white child and denied to the Negro; the latter may not only have less chance to "learn," in the broadest sense; his motivation and sense of well-being may be affected by his inferior status, which will have an adverse effect on his performance. Occasionally all of these handicaps may be overcome; more frequently, improvement occurs *to the extent that* the handicaps are reduced, but the differences cannot be expected to disappear until *all* the handicaps are removed (Klineberg, 1963).

In this connection Marie Jahoda (1960) refers to the shock experienced by the "champions of racial equality" when they learned that Negro children admitted to newly desegregated schools showed an average achievement below that of their white classmates. As she correctly points out, such results should have been expected on the basis of the inferior schooling previously available to most of these Negro children, their lower economic level, and other factors entering into Negro performance. No one can deny that the average Negro achievement is *at present* below the level of the whites. There is no reason to believe, however, that this divergence will continue indefinitely.

In any case, even those psychologists who prefer an explanation in terms of "race" admit that there is *overlapping* whenever two "racial" groups are compared. "Overlapping" is usually defined technically as the percentage in one group that is superior in test scores to the median or average score obtained by the other. In every comparison made in the test scores of Negro and white groups, there is some degree of overlapping. Even the most convinced believer in the superiority of the whites would therefore have to agree that some Negroes do better than the average white. The conclusion is inescapable that any lines of demarcation, political, economic, social, or educational, drawn in such a manner as to separate two "racial" groups on the ground that there is an inborn, permanent superiority of all the members of one group over the other, have no justification in science. This conclusion becomes even stronger if, as the writer is convinced, there is no scientifically acceptable evidence at all in favor of the position that any "racial" group is superior to any other.

This does not mean that heredity plays no part in the determination of behavior. On the contrary, there is good evidence that "individuals" and "families" may be distinguished from others in terms of inherited as well as acquired characteristics. As regards large "racial" groups, however, there appears to be about the same range of hereditary capacities in one group as in another. The fact that differences in behavior between such groups obviously exist, is no proof that they exist because they are inborn.

There is ample reason, therefore, in the light of the accumulated scientific knowledge accepted by the overwhelming majority of social and biological scientists, to concur in the conclusions of the UNESCO Statement on Race:

> According to present knowledge, there is no proof that the groups of mankind differ in their innate mental characteristics, whether in respect of intelligence or temperament. The scientific evidence indicates that the range of mental capacities in all ethnic groups is much the same.

Science thus ranges itself clearly and unmistakably on the side of those who maintain that any political or social action based on "racism" is completely unjustified.

To return to the point from which we started, mythological views of race, and unjustified assumptions of a racial hierarchy, have had a devastating effect on the international scene. If the facts ascertained by psychologists and anthropologists regarding race were more widely known and more generally accepted, the whole world pattern would be changed for the better. Erroneous ideas about race have so far caused much more damage than nuclear bombs. The human factor—in the shape of human error —has on this issue had very real implications indeed for international relations.

It may seem to some that the title of this chapter "The Myth of Race" goes a bit too far. There may be myths *concerning* race (so the argument runs), but surely that does not mean that race itself is a myth. The writer is aware that many geneticists and anthropologists whose opinions he respects continue to use the concept of race and regard it as indispensable in their scientific work. Nor can anyone deny that it is usually possible to distinguish Negroes and Asians from whites, and even, with some degree of success, Englishmen from Germans. Recognition as such, however, is not a satisfactory criterion, since it depends on so many factors—gesture, gait, facial expression, clothes, accent, and so on—that may have nothing to do with inherited characteristics. Conversely, we can distinguish blondes from brunettes and redheads without assuming that therefore there must be three major races according to color of hair. The point is that we have not as yet discovered any acceptable criterion for subdividing mankind. Popular views about race are therefore in a real sense mythological, especially when they assume that people who look different from us *must* necessarily be intellectually and culturally different, and therefore "alien." This is the myth that has poisoned men's minds, led to exploitation and destruction, and bequeathed to the world a legacy of hatred.

There is an allied tendency to which we now turn; namely, the habit of perceiving or judging national groups in terms of stereotypes. In this case, the characteristics are not necessarily ascribed to "race" or considered to be inborn and permanent; they may at the same time shape our contacts and affect our relationships with others to such an extent as to interfere with an objective approach. Stereotypes may therefore create barriers to international understanding and lessen the likelihood of international cooperation.

4

Pictures in Our Heads

If you have a Hungarian for a friend,
you have no need of an enemy.

Old Saying

This unfriendly reference to Hungarians, which the present writer of course does not accept, may be taken as symbolic of a widespread tendency toward a kind of shorthand characterization of whole groups. The judgments expressed in this fashion are usually called "stereotypes," which may succinctly be defined as "pictures in our heads." They are usually widely held; they tend to remain relatively stable and unresponsive to objective facts; and they involve some degree of evaluation of the groups concerned.

Stereotypes may apply to groups of many different varieties. Images may automatically arise when we hear words like "international banker," "trade-union leader," or "male adagio dancer," or when we are told that a young man is a student at Oxford or Harvard. We have certain expectations regarding the personal characteristics or the behavior of those to whom these terms apply. Similarly, we have images, usually shared by many others in the group to which we belong, regarding people of a particular nationality, and most of us appear quite ready to generalize about *the* Scots, *the* Japanese, or *the* Australians. In what follows we shall be particularly concerned with stereotypes as they apply to nations.

Stereotypes are generalizations, but not all generalizations are stereotypes. If we have made a study of a representative sample of trade-union leaders or of Irishmen, and have discovered on the basis of adequate evidence that each one of these groups has certain features that characterize all or nearly all of its members, we have arrived at an inductive generalization, not a stereotype. The special quality of the stereotype is that it is based not on carefully collected data but on hearsay, on anecdotes, on partial and incomplete experience, on what "people" have said. This does not mean that the stereotype is always and necessarily false (we shall return to this problem later), but it does mean that it is taken on faith rather than founded on demonstrated fact.

It is difficult to avoid the stereotyping tendency. There is an obvious temptation to accept convenient short cuts to generalization instead of engaging in the tiring and complex task of acquiring the needed information, and reserving judgment until the individual German or Chinese has demonstrated what he is really like.

Duijker and Frijda (1960) go so far as to argue that stereotyped thinking is inevitable. As they express it, "It scarcely can be denied that stereotypes have the function, which they share with many other kinds of generalizations, of rendering our world more tractable, more manageable. . . . It would be unrealistic to disapprove of stereotyped thinking, for that means disapproval of thinking itself" (p. 125). Even if we cannot rid ourselves and others of this tendency, however, there should at least be awareness of its existence and of its dangers, as well as a willingness to modify our stereotypes in the light of more adequate information. The present writer believes that this is possible, and indeed necessary in order to remove the distortions of perception that would otherwise persist.

Research in many different countries has shown that national or ethnic stereotypes are held and expressed by the large majority of people, and that there may be considerable agreement regarding the characteristics ascribed to particular groups. At an American university (Princeton), in a study conducted by Katz and Braly (1933), out of one hundred students who were the subjects of the investigation, seventy-eight selected for the Germans the adjective "scientifically minded," and sixty-five described them as "industrious"; fifty-three students used the term "artistic" for the Italians; eighty-four regarded Negroes as "superstitious" and seventy-five considered them "lazy"; fifty-three described the English as "sportsmanlike"; seventy-nine agreed that the Jews were "shrewd"; fifty-four that Turks were "cruel." We may describe the results in a slightly different manner by indicating the three or four characteristics most commonly ascribed to each nationality. These included, for the Germans, scientifically minded, industrious, stolid; the Italians, artistic, impulsive, passionate; the Negroes, superstitious, lazy, happy-go-lucky, ignorant; the Irish, pugnacious, quick-tempered, witty; the English, sportsmanlike, intelligent, conventional; the Jews, shrewd, mercenary, industrious; the Americans, industrious, intelligent, materialistic, ambitious; the Chinese, superstitious, sly, conservative; the Japanese, intelligent, industrious, progressive; the Turks, cruel, religious, treacherous. A study conducted in Japan in 1936 showed that there were four adjectives applied to the Japanese —industrious, imitative, suave, and neat—on which the Japanese and American university students were in almost complete agreement. It is not surprising that the Japanese did not use words like shrewd, sly, treacherous, and aggressive, to describe their own people; it is perhaps less clear why they did not accept such words as intelligent, progressive, quiet, and alert, which also figured prominently among those chosen by the Americans (Kusunoki, 1936).

In 1952, German students at the Free University of Berlin gave somewhat similar responses. Americans were described as democratic and materialistic; Italians as passionate and musical; Chinese as poor, modest, inscrutable; Germans as conscientious, patriotic, intelligent; the English as patriotic, conservative, and sportsmanlike (Sodhi and Bergius, 1953).

In 1948 and 1949 a study was conducted under UNESCO auspices in nine countries, in each of which a representative sample of about 1000 persons served as subjects. They were all given a list of twelve adjectives, from which they were asked to choose those that applied to themselves, to Americans, to Russians, and in some instances to two or three other national groups as well. The adjectives chosen most frequently by the British subjects to describe Americans were: progressive, conceited, generous, peace-loving, intelligent, and practical; Americans thought of the British as intelligent, industrious, courageous, peace-loving, conceited, and self-controlled. All the groups studied were in agreement on one point: their own nation was the most peace-loving of all! (Buchanan and Cantril, 1953).

Where do national stereotypes come from? How do they originate? It has been suggested that one source may be the language we speak, which through the use of common expressions with an ethnic referent may contribute to the tendency to attribute specific characteristics to ethnic groups. English appears to be particularly rich in such expressions. For example, we find the following, which are presented as a sampling from what is undoubtedly a much larger linguistic universe:

Dutch treat—when each person pays his own way.

Dutch courage—which is fortified by alcohol.

Dutch uncle—who gives advice or instruction strictly and severely.

Double Dutch—completely incomprehensible.

His fine Italian hand—really subtle, devious, perhaps a bit Machiavellian.

A Chinese puzzle—very complicated.

To take French leave—to slip away quietly, when no one is watching. Interestingly enough, the French say *"filer à l'anglaise"* for exactly the same behavior; the Italians also do it "like the English" (*filarse a l'inglesa*).

To Jew him down—to bargain in order to get a lower price.

Nigger in the woodpile—something unexpected, usually some double dealing or "dirty work."

Working like a nigger—really hard work.

There are comparable ethnic references in other languages, as has been indicated above. Italians say *"fare il portughese,"* to do what the Portuguese do, when they refer to slipping into a theater or onto a streetcar without paying the price of admission, or otherwise "getting away with it." A Frenchman who prefaces his remarks by the statement *"Je suis un paysan du Danube"* (I am a peasant from the Danube) means that he is ignorant of the subject on which he is about to speak. The Chinese of course have different written characters for different countries; the ones used for the United States may be Romanized as *mei kuo,* which means "beautiful country." (Some American missionary may have been able to make his influence felt at an early stage.) As a matter of fact, the Chinese characters for nations are generally favorable. Certain unfriendly expressions used for Manchus and other neighbors were "cleaned up" in the eighteenth century. On the other hand, the expression "foreign devils" or "ocean devils" (*Yang kuei tzu*) is still popularly used, or was until recently, for white men in general.

It is difficult to determine just how great an influence is exerted by such expressions, or whether they are simply the reflection of stereotypes that are already widely accepted. A similar problem emerges with regard to the ethnic jokes or anecdotes that may often have a wide circulation. The writer remembers that during his childhood in Canada it was assumed that the Englishman had no sense of humor. As an example of the stories told, there was one that went approximately as follows: "How can you make an Englishman happy in his old age?" The answer was to "tell him a really good story when he's young!" Brazilians have an extensive collection of stories about the Portuguese, who are usually pictured as slow, good-natured, well-meaning but rather stupid individuals. One sample tells of a Brazilian woman who enters a crowded streetcar and is very much annoyed because none of the men get up to give her a seat. "What lack of breeding!" she repeats over and over again. Finally the little Portuguese looks up at her and says sweetly, "It's not breeding we lack, Madam. It's just seats!" A collection of such stories from many lands would not only be amusing, but might also reveal something significant regarding the variations in the stereotypes held in different places in relation to the same ethnic group.

The question of cause and effect also arises in connection with the suggestion that the mass media—newspapers, magazines, books, the cinema, and more recently, television—represent a significant source of ethnic stereotypes. Most probably the relation is a circular one, with the mass media reflecting stereotypes already in the public domain, and at the same time giving them a wider dissemination and additional credence. In any case, there can be no doubt that stereotypes find their way into many of the popular media of entertainment. The present writer, who has a weakness for detective fiction, has come across frequent expressions of this type: "with typical German thoroughness," "broke through his English reserve," "smouldering Latin temperament," "Chinese indirection," "American optimism," "Scottish taciturnity," "Indian (American) stoicism." This list could be extended almost indefinitely.

On a much more objective level, a study was made of the content of one-hundred ninety-eight short stories published in eight of the most widely read magazines in the United States in 1937 and 1943. A quantitative analysis of the stories and of the characters in them showed substantial differences in the treatment of "Americans" and members of minority or foreign groups. The authors of the study state that fully three fourths of the minority and foreign characters were described along the lines of widely diffused stereotypes. Examples included the amusingly ignorant Negro, the Italian gangster, the sly and shrewd Jew, the emotional Irishman, the primitive and backward Pole, the patronized native of a Pacific island. Americans represented "approved" characters more frequently than did foreigners; among the latter, those of Anglo-Saxon or Nordic origin represented "approved" characters quite often, whereas other foreign groups were found to a disproportionate degree among the "disapproved" characters. The Americans also enjoyed higher socioeconomic status and had more desirable occupations than the other groups. Americans more frequently pursued ideals, while the others sought material goals. The authors conclude that magazine fiction would increase the tendencies to assign stereotypic descriptions to foreign groups and give readers the impression that they had found "proof" for their stereotypes (Berelson and Salter, 1946).

It is highly probable that a similar study of American magazine fiction today would indicate a marked reduction in this stereotyping tendency with regard to many ethnic groups, although there may possibly have been a corresponding increase in connection with national groups identified as opponents in the Cold War. In the American cinema there also appears to have been a conscious effort to do away with the stereotyping of minority groups, but there has not been quite so much concern with the image of "foreigners." In any case it must be remembered that eliminating stereotypes in the mass media now will still leave a large proportion of the population that has been exposed to them in the fairly recent past. It will take time for the new trend to make itself felt.

A problem of special concern to the educator arises out of the presence of national stereotypes in the schoolbooks used by children, particularly in history and geography. A number of studies based on an analysis of the content of such schoolbooks has revealed this tendency to be present to a marked degree. One such study examined the treatment of the same wars and battles by American historians and by those of former enemy countries, including the United Kingdom, Canada, Spain, Mexico, and Germany. The authors in *all* countries are substantially in agreement that the leaders of their own country were honorable, and their soldiers noble and courageous; when defeated it was because of the overwhelming force of the enemy; the enemy, whatever his identity, was treacherous and cowardly, and one's own army heroic and brave (Walworth, 1938). As far as relations between Asians and Europeans are concerned, western schoolbooks are apparently characterized not only by the tendency to stereotype the Oriental, but also to pay much too little attention to people and events far from the western scene. In this whole area of school textbooks much progress has recently been made, particularly under the auspices of UNESCO, but here again one must be prepared for a considerable time lag before these improvements can be expected to have a salutary effect.

These few examples by no means exhaust the range and variety of possible causes of ethnic stereotypes. It is clear also that stereotypes serve the function of rationalizing or justifying our treatment of other groups. If our image of the Negro is that he makes a good servant but not an effective teacher or doctor, we will be less prepared to give him equality of opportunity with whites. In the case of the Chinese on the West Coast of the United States, this mechanism has been clearly demonstrated. When the Chinese were needed in California—because the white migrants from other parts of the United States were so anxious to get rich quickly that they had no patience with domestic labor or with work in the cigar factories—the Chinese were welcome. During that period newspapers and journals referred to them as among "the most worthy of our newly adopted citizens," "the best immigrants in California"; they were spoken of as thrifty, sober, tractable, inoffensive, law-abiding. They showed an "all-round ability" and an "adaptability beyond praise." This flattering picture prevailed during a considerable period. Then around the 1860s, when the economic situation had changed and other groups were competing with the Chinese for the positions they were occupying, there was a corresponding change in the stereotype of the Chinese. In the elections of 1867 both political parties introduced into their platforms legislation "protecting" Californians against Mongolian competition. The phrases now applied to the Chinese included: "a distinct people," "unassimilable," "their presence lowered the plane of living," "they shut out white labor." They were spoken of as clannish, criminal, debased and servile, deceitful and vicious; they smuggled opium; Chinatowns were full of prostitution and gambling; the Chinese were filthy and loathsome in their habits, undesirable as workers and residents in the country (Shrieke, 1936).

This startling change in the "characteristics" of the Chinese can hardly be accounted for by any change in the nature of the Chinese population of California. The only acceptable explanation is that the change in economic conditions there made it advantageous for the whites to try to eliminate the Chinese from economic competition, and the stereotype was altered in a direction that would help to justify such action.

Leaving the question of the causes of stereotypes, what about their effects? On the one hand it has been argued that national stereotypes do not themselves affect international relations but merely reflect them. It has been pointed out, for example, that before World War II the American stereotype of the Turks was unfavorable and that of the Germans exceedingly friendly, but that in the war Americans and Turks were allied against Germany. The content of the American image of the Japanese was quite different before, during, and after the war, respectively, changing with the pattern of political events.

There is certainly a great deal of merit in this view, but a case could also be made for its opposite. It is at least conceivable that the stereotypes held by Germans before World War II contributed in substantial degree to their warlike attitude and their preparations for war. The opinions held by many Germans concerning the Poles and Russians, for example, were by no means unimportant in preparing the way for a German attack against these peoples. It might be argued with considerable plausibility that the opinions held by Hitler concerning the fighting qualities and the powers of resistance of the Russians and the British were in part responsible for his decision to run the risk of fighting on two fronts. It was because he thought, erroneously as it turned out, that both the Russians and the British would quickly give in, that he felt himself in a position to gamble as he did. A good case might be made for the view that if Hitler had recognized the real qualities of his enemies, instead of being misled by false and inadequate stereotypes, he might have made very different decisions, and the whole course of history might have been affected thereby. This analysis is admittedly speculative, but is sufficiently plausible to be used as an argument in favor of the notion that the existence of such stereotypes may play an important part in determining acts that lead to, or away from, war.

At a more experimental and objective level, it is possible to demonstrate that the existence of a stereotype may actually affect our perception of the group concerned. In one such study, the

technique used was that known as the method of "serial reproduction." A slide was thrown upon a screen, usually a semidra-
matic picture containing a large number of related details. The
experimenter described the picture to the first subject, who could
not himself see the screen. A second subject entered the room,
and the first subject proceeded to tell him all he could about the
picture. This was continued through a chain of six or seven subjects. One picture represented a subway scene in which two of
the passengers are conversing; one of them is a Negro and the
other a white man in working clothes. The white man is holding
an open razor in his left hand. In over half of the experiments with
this picture, the final reproduction located the razor in the hand
of the Negro; in some cases the Negro was even reported as
"brandishing" it, or as "threatening" the white man with it. It
seems clear that the widespread acceptance of the stereotype that
the Negro uses a razor as a weapon is responsible for this result.
This does not mean that half the subjects reacted in such a fashion, since one such shift in a rumor chain might be reproduced by
all who followed. It does mean that in 50 percent of the *groups*
this phenomenon was observed. There were two striking exceptions to this finding. When Negro subjects were used, there was
no such distortion, for obvious reasons; nor did it occur in young
children, who had not yet learned the stereotype (Allport and
Postman, 1947).

In another investigation, a group of college students was shown
photographs of thirty girls and asked to rank each photograph on
a five-point scale, indicating their general liking of the girl, her
beauty, her intelligence, her character, her ambition, and her
"entertainingness." Two months later, the subjects were again
shown the same photographs, but with surnames added. For
some of the photographs Jewish surnames were given, such as
Rabinowitz, Finkelstein; a second group received Italian surnames such as Scarano, Grisolia; a third received Irish surnames
such as McGillicuddy, O'Shaughnessy; and a fourth, "old American" names like Adams and Clark. The results demonstrated that
the mere labeling of the photographs with these various surnames
had a definite effect upon the manner in which the photographs
were perceived. The addition of Jewish and Italian surnames, for

example, resulted in a substantial drop in general liking, and a smaller drop in ratings for beauty and character; it also resulted in a rise in the ratings for ambition, more marked in the case of the Jewish surnames. It seems clear that in these cases the stereotypes associated with ethnic groups had a very definite effect upon the perception of the photographs, and upon the consequent judgment of the characteristics possessed by these girls. Other examples could be added of this tendency to see what we expect to see, or what fits in with our preconceptions. The stereotype definitely affects our perception (Razran, 1950).

The instances just cited all indicate the effect of the stereotypes on those who hold them. What about the people regarding whom they are held, the *stereotypee* rather than the *stereotyper?* Here there are no objective studies with which the writer is familiar, but one or two personal experiences may at least be suggestive. In theory, the effect could work in two different directions. On the one hand, the stereotyped group might be moved to act in the direction expected of them. There is evidence that southern Negroes will occasionally take on the "folk" characteristics attributed to them, when dealing with whites who occupy a superior position. To take another example, a French friend once informed the writer that when he attended an international conference, he was much more excitable, voluble, and "Latin" than when he was with other Frenchmen. "Otherwise," he said, "my Anglo-Saxon friends would be disappointed." In a recent book by André Maurois, *The Life of Sir Alexander Fleming,* the discoverer of penicillin is described in these words: "He knew what his behavior was supposed to be: that of a taciturn Scot, and he conscientiously played up to it."

On the other hand, there may be the opposite effect because of the feeling that the stereotype ought to be proved wrong. A Scot or a Jew may be particularly generous and even a spendthrift, because his group is regarded as especially careful about money; a Negro may refuse to sing, claiming that he is unable to keep a tune; a Latin American may keep his appointments—at least with North Americans—exactly on the dot, because he is expected to arrive late. All we have here is a series of anecdotes; we need more objective data. It seems clear, however, that groups about whom stereotypes are held will frequently modify their own behavior as a result.

We turn now to a problem to which brief reference was made above, that of the truth or falsity of the stereotype. Some writers use the word as if it necessarily meant a false generalization. Others, on the contrary, appear to believe that the very existence of a stereotype proves that it contains at least some truth, an argument analogous to the proverbial "where there's smoke there's fire." This in turn is akin to the popular impression that if *everybody* (or nearly everybody) agrees that the Irish are pugnacious, the Scots parsimonious, and the Chinese sly, surely it must be true.

Research has demonstrated, however, that stereotypes *can* and *do* develop without any basis in reality. One investigator analyzed the attitudes of six-hundred-ten non-Armenians toward first- and second-generation Armenian immigrants in Fresno County, California. There was almost complete agreement that the Armenians in California had more than their share of faults, and the general attitude toward them was relatively unfriendly. The investigator proceeded to question the non-Armenians as to the reasons for their antipathies, and he was able to classify the answers in three distinct categories of stereotypes. In the first place it was stated that the Armenians were dishonest, lying, deceitful. In actual fact, when measured by the criterion of business integrity, the Armenians turned out to be equal, and frequently superior, to non-Armenians. In the second place, Armenians were alleged to be parasites and not to contribute their share to community life and welfare. Actually, the Armenian demands upon free clinics and hospitals were less than half of what would be expected in terms of their proportion of the population; the same held true for social-work cases. Finally, it was stated that the Armenians had an inferior code of morality, and that their behavior led to frequent cases of social and legal friction. In fact, the police records showed that the Armenians appeared in only 1.5 percent of police court cases although they constituted approximately 6 percent of the population. The conclusion was that these stereotypes have one factor in common; they are all false (LaPiere, 1936).

Indirect but convincing evidence in the same direction is furnished by another study, which was concerned with the occurrence of stereotypes related to proper names. In one part of the study, one-hundred-twenty male subjects were asked to "match" eight masculine names with eight personal characteristics. The results to be expected by chance alone, that is to say, if no stereotypes existed, would be 120 divided by 8, or 15 for each name. The actual results showed that 63 out of 120 judges matched Richard with good-looking; 104 agreed that Cuthbert was a "sissy"; 58 judged Herman to be stupid; 59 said that Rex was athletic; 71 judged Adrian to be artistic. In a similar experiment with girls judging feminine names, 54 regarded Minnie as stupid; 60 thought that Maisie was talkative; and 73 said that Agatha was middle-aged. It seems highly probable that comparable stereotypes would be found in languages other than English and in groups other than American students.

These stereotypes obviously have causes, but these may be found in characterizations that occur in novels or the cinema rather than in any actual experience. It could, perhaps, be argued that the reason that Agatha is so often regarded as middle-aged is because it was a common name a generation ago but has now lost favor, so that the Agathas one actually meets do tend on the whole to be older than the average. This is a possibility, but it is difficult to find a similar explanation for the fact that Richard is good-looking, or Minnie stupid. Even though these particular stereotypes do not apply to national groups, the study demonstrates that stereotypes may develop without any "kernel of truth," and the results therefore have relevance to the field of stereotypes in general (Schoenfeld, 1942).

Still another argument against the notion that stereotypes always contain some truth is furnished by the fact that they may be self-contradictory. One aspect of the stereotype of the Jews, for instance, is that they are too clannish, that they keep to themselves in closed communities, and do not join with others in common activities. This judgment may be held simultaneously with its opposite; that is, that they constantly push themselves forward into non-Jewish groups even when they are not wanted. Obviously these two comments on Jewish behavior cannot both be true at the same time for Jews in general, even though the first could be true of some Jews, and the second of others. As Duijker and Frijda express it, there is here "a peaceful coexistence of mutually incompatible convictions" (*op. cit.,* p. 117).

This does *not* mean that stereotypes are always false; it does mean that they *may* be. The danger arises out of the fact that we use them, often blindly and automatically, without really knowing anything about their truth. To the educator, this represents a widespread tendency against which students must be warned, namely, that of generalizing without adequate evidence. One difficulty is that we do not always possess the "adequate evidence" regarding national characteristics that can be used as a corrective against the exaggerations or distortions of the stereotype. Research in this whole field has been proceeding actively, but a great deal remains to be accomplished (Chapter 13).

This raises a further question—whether anything can be done to eliminate, or at least reduce, the use of national stereotypes. Certainly the educational task involved is not an easy one, and the providing of relevant information will not always suffice. We know, on the basis of much research as well as common-sense observation, that our perceptions do not necessarily mirror the external reality with which we are presented. In the first place, we *select,* we pay attention only to certain parts of that reality; if we believe the Italians are noisy, we may defend our stereotype by noticing those who are, and ignoring those who are not. Secondly, we *distort,* as when we transfer the open razor from the white man to the Negro. Thirdly, we *reinterpret,* so that the same behavior may literally be seen as different depending on its source. It has been said that the in-group's virtues may be the out-group's vices; ambition is good in one of *us,* but a danger in one of *them.* This tendency is perhaps most aptly expressed in the phrase: "I am firm, you are stubborn, he is pig-headed," in which the same behavior is placed in differing frames of reference. Finally—though other mechanisms may also operate—we can *dismiss as exceptions* those members of a national group who are brought to our attention as disproving our stereotypes, and no one has yet demonstrated how many cases may be considered exceptions.

All of this make the educational task difficult, but not hopeless or impossible. Under certain conditions of personal experience, for example, stereotypes can be changed or reduced. This was demonstrated in a study conducted under UNESCO auspices among schoolchildren in London. The investigators began by recording the opinions held by these children concerning various ethnic groups, particularly African Negroes. They were then placed in contact with two excellent African schoolteachers, who spent several weeks in the schools. The changes that occurred were striking, and the more favorable opinions that developed usually extended to other "foreign" groups as well (James and Tenen, 1953). In the United States, contact between Negroes and whites in the armed forces as well as in interracial housing projects has also had the effect of reducing the tendency to stereotype. This does not mean that similar results can always be anticipated, but the outlook is promising for comparable experiences among other ethnic groups.

Reference was made above to a 1932 study of the stereotypes held by students at Princeton University. Eighteen years later, in 1950, the study was repeated, and the investigator noted a striking change which he described as a "fading effect." There was in general much less agreement among the students in 1950 than in 1932; any specific trait was usually checked by a much smaller proportion of students in the later study, even though there was little change in the characteristics that were most frequently attributed. The percentage of students who described Negroes as lazy dropped from 84 percent in 1932 to 31 percent; those describing the Jews as shrewd dropped from 79 percent to 47 percent. The description of Italians as artistic dropped from 83 percent to 28 percent, of the Japanese as industrious from 43 percent to 12 percent, of the Americans as progressive from 27 percent to 5 percent. The investigator concludes that there has been a very marked reduction in the extent to which these stereotypes prevail, as well as in the willingness of the university students to generalize about ethnic groups. He suggests a number of possible reasons for this change—among others, the gradual disappearance of stereotyped characterizations in all entertainment and communication media. Perhaps even more important in this context, he expresses the belief that the observed decrease in stereotyped thinking may be due in part to the effect of college courses in the social sciences; these have introduced caution and a critical attitude toward ethnic generalizations (Gilbert, 1951).

To the extent that this is true, it gives us hope for the role of social science and education in providing a more objective framework for our relations with other peoples, in replacing hearsay by hard facts, and stereotypes by scientific knowledge of national characteristics. Although this task may be a difficult one, there can be little doubt about its importance. International relations are, at least in part, carried on by people of different nationalities who meet around the conference table, in diplomatic exchanges, as members of technical assistance missions, within the framework of United Nations activities, and so forth. It is inevitable that they will bring with them the accumulated stereotyped opinions that are commonly accepted in their own country. This will determine them to behave in certain ways in dealing with foreign nationals, and to expect certain forms of behavior from them in return. If these stereotypes are inaccurate and misleading, they may contribute to misunderstanding and consequent failure in the conduct of international affairs. The first necessary step would seem to be an awareness of the existence of the stereotypes and of their uncertain quality; this may in turn lead to a more realistic assessment of the characteristics of others (see Chapter 13).

Stereotypes may be regarded as the *cognitive* aspect of our relations with other groups, the ideas and opinions we hold concerning them. The term "attitudes" has been used to refer to affective or emotional components, our feelings for or against others, as well as to our readiness for certain forms of behavior. The distinction is difficult to maintain, however, since opinions and attitudes are usually closely allied. The following discussion of attitudes should therefore be considered as an extension of the contents of the present chapter.

CHAPTER

5

"I Hate Everybody"

*I hate everybody, irrespective of race,
creed, color or national origin.*

The New Yorker

This caption appeared some time ago in a *New Yorker* cartoon in which a man in a bar, who has evidently had too much to drink, in this manner declares his hostility against the whole world. It may be regarded as expressing the essential point of this chapter, namely that our attitudes, particularly in the field of intergroup and international relations, are frequently based on irrational, subjective factors.

This is a difficult conclusion for most people to accept. In connection with stereotypes, reference was made to the common assumption that if *everybody* says the Irish are pugnacious or the Jews mercenary, surely this must be true. In the present context, the argument usually takes the form of certainty that, if *I* like Norwegians or dislike Turks, surely they must deserve it. The possibility that one may not only be wrong but irrational in one's attitudes is rarely conceded.

The writer is not suggesting by any means that all judgments of other ethnic groups are incorrect. As Allport (1954) has wisely insisted, we should whenever possible check such judgments against the facts before we dismiss them as unreasonable or biased. There may be something to the notion of the "well-deserved reputation," to use Allport's phrase, at least in certain cases. At the same time it can be and has been demonstrated that attitudes toward other groups frequently develop in a fashion incompatible with the belief that the groups' behavior is responsible for, and justifies the existence of our attitudes.

In an investigation more than twenty years ago, Murphy and Likert (1938) were able to demonstrate that various ethnic hostilities were usually associated. Those individuals, for example, who were anti-Negro tended also to be anti-Jewish and against "foreigners" in general. This finding was corroborated in a later large-scale study of *The Authoritarian Personality* (Adorno *et al.,* 1950), which also delved deeply into the personal characteristics of those who showed a high degree of prejudice or "ethnocentrism." Similarly, Hartley (1946) was able to demonstrate that these attitudes clustered together. He made use of the Bogardus Social Distance Scale, in which subjects are asked, quite literally, at what "distance" from themselves they would like to keep other ethnic groups. The greatest "distance" was to keep them out of the country, and the smallest was to accept them as members of one's own family through intermarriage; there were seven possible degrees of distance altogether. His results indicate that among the students who were examined, when an attitude of unfriendliness toward "foreigners" developed, it was usually extended indiscriminately ("I hate everybody!"). His analysis included responses to thirty-two different ethnic groups; he divided these into two lists, "odd" and "even," and computed "tolerance scores" based on the amount of social distance shown toward the two sets of groups separately. There was a remarkably high degree of correspondence; that is, those students who showed little distance toward the one list, also, with few exceptions, accepted the other; those who rejected one half of the groups also usually rejected the other half. Such results show it cannot be the behavior of the ethnic groups that is responsible for the attitudes shown toward them, but rather something in the students themselves.

The irrationality of these attitudes is shown even more clearly in a second portion of Hartley's study. In addition to the thirty-two groups mentioned above, he included in his list the names of three imaginary peoples (he called them the "non-such" groups). These were the Danerians, the Wallonians, and the Pirenians. Some of the students refused to indicate at what distance from themselves they would keep these groups on the ground that they knew nothing about them, but the majority evidently found no great difficulty in answering the question. As a matter of fact, there was considerable rejection of these groups! More important, and again with relatively few exceptions, those who showed a high degree of tolerance for the *real* groups also accepted the imaginary ones, and conversely. The "well-deserved reputation" can hardly enter here; no one had ever been attacked by a Danerian or robbed by a Wallonian. There can be no doubt about the irrationality of these attitudes.

Where, then, do they come from? The discussion of the causes of stereotypes in the preceding chapter is relevant to this issue; as a matter of fact stereotypes and attitudes really represent two parts of the same complex phenomenon. As has already been indicated, stereotypes in this context refer to what we think or believe about certain nations, and attitudes, to our feelings and our "set" toward them, our readiness to behave in certain ways. The relation between these two aspects is not quite perfect. One *can* accept the stereotype of Negro inferiority and yet give every opportunity to individual Negroes; one *can* dislike Jews in general and also assert with complete honesty the cliché about "some of my best friends."

It remains true that most of the time, and for most people, the relationship between attitudes and opinions is a very close one. What was said in Chapter 4 about the effects of linguistic expressions, stories and anecdotes, portrayal of ethnic groups in the mass media, and so forth, applies equally well in the case of attitudes. The additional analysis that follows is also directed toward the understanding of the causes of the whole attitude-opinion complex.

The evidence reviewed above has led a number of investigators to conclude that personality factors, frequently of a deep-seated, unconscious character, play an important part. Research on *The Authoritarian Personality*, for example, showed the ethnocentric individual to have the following characteristics, among others: he is a conformist, he sees the world as menacing and unfriendly, he exalts his own group, he is fundamentally anxious and insecure, he blames others for his own faults and misfortunes, he appears to worship his parents but has strong repressed hostility against them. This description applies particularly to the individual who is prejudiced against minority groups, but in view of the fact that such prejudice is usually accompanied by hostility against foreigners, it may be considered equally applicable to the field of international relations.

The psychological instrument that contributed to the above findings is known as the F Scale, the "F" referring to the fact that the characteristics it reveals are closely allied to Fascist ideology. A very large amount of subsequent research has uncovered certain defects and raised some serious methodological questions about the F Scale, but on the whole the conclusions to which it has led are considered sound as far as they go (Christie and Cook, 1958). The major criticism is the relative neglect of social and cultural factors, as distinct from personality variables, in the shaping of attitudes.

The importance of cultural pressures is brought out clearly in a study conducted in the South by Pettigrew (1958). Although the southern subjects showed themselves to be considerably more anti-Negro than the northerners, they were not more authoritarian; that is, they did not obtain higher scores on the F Scale. This means that the difference between North and South in the attitudes toward Negroes cannot be attributed to personality, but rather to regional culture. Similarly, the differences in the attitudes of Brazilians and South Africans toward Negroes, or of residents of Hawaii and California toward Orientals, is much more a matter of culture than of personality. It still seems certain, however, that *within* each of these groups the variations found among individuals, all of whom have been exposed to approximately the same system of cultural norms and values, will best be explained on the basis of personality.

There have been many attempts to define more directly the relation between warlike attitudes and personality characteristics. Stagner (1955), for example, reports that students who readily accepted war as an instrument of national policy also had more "aggressive" attitudes in other areas, including a favorable reaction to capital punishment, to the use of force in interpersonal relations, and the like. A study in Norway (Christiansen, 1959) suggests that destructive tendencies in international affairs are inversely related to willingness to take the responsibility oneself for solving everyday conflicts. More recently Scott (1960) has indicated that there is a positive, though small, amount of correspondence between one's international goals and one's personal goals; the kind of international relations that the subjects advocate can to some degree be predicted from a knowledge of their personal values. These investigations, and others like them, have by no means answered all the questions concerned with the personal causes of the attitudes to one's own and other nations, but they have demonstrated that such causes play a part.

Another of the findings of *The Authoritarian Personality* is relevant in this connection. Those persons who were most prejudiced against minority groups and foreigners also ranked high on a "patriotism" scale—they showed excessive "patriotic" responses. The investigators point out that:

> The term "patriotism" as used here does not mean "love of country." Rather, the present concept involves blind attachment to certain national cultural values, uncritical conformity with the prevailing group ways, and rejection of other nations as outgroups. It might better be termed *pseudopatriotism*. (p. 107).

The problem is to distinguish this extreme chauvinistic nationalism, hyperpatriotism, from its more acceptable counterpart. Loyalty to one's own group frequently brings out the best in man; it may be functional in the sense of contributing to group survival and cooperation. It is at the same time a potential source of many varieties of conflict, including war. Is there anything that we can say about the nature of nationalism, its virtues and its excesses? Huxley and Haddon (1935) point out that: "A 'nation' has been cynically but not inaptly defined as a society united by a common error as to its origin and a common aversion to its neighbors" (p. 5). This may be an extreme statement, but what seems clear is that nationalism exists in the minds of men, and that its influence upon the course of events will depend upon the meaning those minds give to it.

This may seem to be an example of a narrowly psychological viewpoint, but it is reflected in the writings of a number of scholars not identified with the discipline of psychology. The political scientist Graham Wallas (1929) writes: "The modern state exists *as an entity of the mind,* a symbol." The historian Hans Kohn (1948) states that nationalism is *"a state of mind.* The process of history can be analyzed as a succession of changes in communal *psychology,* in the *attitudes of man* toward the manifestations of individual and social life" (p. 18, italics supplied).

Although nationalism, therefore, is an attitude subject to the same kind of developmental history as other attitudes, with a similar interpenetration of rational and irrational factors, it has the special quality that it is not only *for* something but almost always at the same time *against* something else. Long ago it was suggested that an "in-group" is always contrasted with an "out-group." This does not seem to be essential, but it helps! Gunnar Myrdal (1952) points out that in none of the existing national cultures are people educated to know and like people in other countries who are different from themselves; on the contrary, they are often indoctrinated with national self-righteousness and are apt to despise, fear, and hate those who are outside the nation and live differently. "The joining with others in showing dislikes and the standing together in voicing threats and recriminations against other nations actually increase the individual's subjective experience of national 'belongingness' and are therefore felt to be unifying moral forces in the people." It is not surprising that, particularly in times of stress, those who are in a position to determine what is said to the people will exaggerate the hateful qualities of a potential "enemy" in order to solidify unity and support at home. The dangers of such procedure in connection with international relations are obvious; propaganda of this type may be disastrous.

We learn the nationalism that is taught to us—at home, in school, or through the mass media. In addition we select certain items from what is presented to us and distort others, so that we "learn" what is congruent with the needs of our personality. It is in this process that irrational factors may play their part. As Scott (1958) expresses it, even "the first step toward rationality" will probably not be taken by most people, "since the realm of foreign affairs is generally remote from their most pressing concerns"; as a consequence, "international attitudes may frequently be characterized by non-rationality of various forms."

Part of the nonrationality seems to be due, however, to lack of knowledge related to lack of interest; this means that educational experiences directed toward the modification of national attitudes in order to prepare the way for international collaboration may make a difference. This is the belief that underlies many of UNESCO's activities such as its educational programs related to the mutual cultural appreciation of east and west, to "Education for International Understanding," to knowledge of national characteristics, to the reduction of racism, to the improvement of school textbooks in history and geography by the elimination of unfriendly references to other nations, to the development of confidence in the United Nations.

The question of the nature of nationalism and its influence on international affairs is a complicated one that has been studied in great detail by historians and political scientists; it also has economic aspects of fundamental importance. There is perhaps not a great deal psychologists can add, but the following considerations may be of some potential assistance:

1. The nonrational character of at least some aspects of our nationalist attitudes has been amply demonstrated. The first important step would be the recognition of the nature of these attitudes, and a knowledge of our own motives and values in relation to them. As Stagner (1946) puts it,

> Self-insight is integrally related to the preservation of world peace because it is only with insight that reason

achieves control of individual behavior. A man who lacks understanding of his own emotions easily falls prey to propaganda . . . he may be induced to project aggression onto foreign peoples and . . . acts in an irrational manner.

2. Nations consist of groups of people, and the knowledge of the nature of groups, acquired through the disciplines of social psychology and sociology may give some hints regarding the functions they perform. "Groups in general are organized to meet human needs: their structures and processes are in part molded by these needs." Guetzkow (1957), from whom these words are quoted, suggests that at the level of the nation, the group fulfills economic, sociocultural, and political needs; the last including security, group loyalty, and prestige. All of these he regards as universal, although their strength will vary in different nations and in different individuals. The question then arises as to what happens when the nation can no longer satisfy these needs, for example, the need for security.

3. Under such circumstances, there is at least the possibility that people may be willing to sacrifice to a supranational body the prestige that goes with complete national sovereignty in return for a guarantee of security. Toward the end of World War II, such willingness was fairly widespread. A majority of Americans questioned in 1943, and an even larger majority of the British, were at that time prepared to give up a limited amount of national sovereignty in order to build a strong and effective international organization (Bruner, 1945). Since that time nationalistic sentiment has undoubtedly increased throughout the world, and it is unlikely that any substantial proportion of the people would now express such willingness. While it is true, however, that attitudes help shape the international political situation, they are also in turn shaped by it. If the threat of nuclear annihilation becomes greater and more apparent, is there an increased likelihood that people will be more ready to extend some of their loyalty from national to international symbols?

We shall return to this problem in another context, but there is an important issue requiring consideration at this point. Discussion has so far concerned itself with the stereotypes and attitudes, many of them dangerously irrational, held by people generally. Are these really important? Do they play any effective role compared with the attitudes and opinions of leaders? What can we say about the nature of leadership in connection with international relations?

6

Follow the Leader

*Let me go, let me go! I must follow those
people! I am their leader!*

From a story relating to an uprising
in Paris in 1848.

This story may be taken as representative of one extreme
position; namely, that the leader is not really different from
those who are led, that although he occupies a special position,
his role is to stay with his followers and give expression to their
needs and their values. At the other extreme there is the view
that the leader is all-important, bending his followers to his will,
shaping their ideas and determining their behavior. The popular
view in connection with politics is probably closer to the second
of these two positions; a majority of Americans would almost
certainly agree that the Russian people are all right, or would be
if they were not led astray by their leaders. As far as can be
ascertained, most Russians would express similar views about
the Americans and their leaders. Apart from the value judgment
involved, this position usually assumes that there is something
special about the leader, that he has certain characteristic quali-

ties that result in his seeking and finding status as a leader, and that others follow him because he possesses those qualities.

This intriguing idea, consonant with what is sometimes described as the "great man" theory of history, for a long time dominated the thinking of psychologists concerned with the problem of leadership. A great many investigations were conducted, the purpose of which was to isolate and describe leadership qualities, to determine *the* characteristics of *the* leader. In spite of the devotion of considerable research energy, this approach led to a dead end. One survey (Bird, 1940) found a total of seventy-nine different traits attributed to leaders in twenty studies; only twenty-eight of these traits appeared in more than one list. This lack of agreement has been corroborated in other reviews, so that most students of this question would agree that the attempt has failed.

There are probably two main reasons for this failure. The first is that research has been directed toward leadership in a wide variety of different situations that may have little or nothing in common with one another. It is not reasonable to assume that the same qualities will emerge in the study of leaders of such disparate groups as kindergarten children, clubs of young boys or girls, college fraternities, units of the armed forces, athletic teams, work crews in industrial establishments. Secondly, there are also variations in the criteria used for the definition of leadership. One valuable survey (Gibb, 1954) distinguishes a number of different ways in which the term has been used. The leader may be an individual in a given office, as the chairman of a committee or the president of a company; he may be the focus for the behavior of group members, the one to whom others address their remarks or whom they seek to convince; he may be the one chosen as leader by others, but in this case choice may depend on whether the task is to solve an intellectual problem or to find one's way through a thick forest, and so on. The person who engages in leadership behavior is not necessarily the one elected to high office, as when the secretary of an international conference subtly but unmistakably channels the discussion through appropriate whispers in the ear of the chairman. A well-known literary example of such variations is found in the play by J. M. Barrie, *The Admirable Crichton,* in which the butler, who previously had obeyed the orders of others, suddenly finds himself the leader, and is accepted as such, under the special conditions imposed by the need for survival on a desert island.

Leadership, therefore, varies in its character depending on the situation and on the group to be led. Different characteristics will be important depending on the nature of the specific social field. This does not mean that personal factors will play no part. Intelligence, for example, is certainly of value to the leader, and there is evidence to the effect that the leader is usually more intelligent than his followers; at the same time, he must not be too far removed from the rest of the group. In other words, intelligence is valued, but within certain limits that are set by the followers. An obvious consequence is that different levels of intelligence will be required and valued in connection with leadership in different groups. An "egghead" may aspire to the presidency of a learned society, but not so easily to an elective political office.

As so often happens, the truth lies somewhere between the extreme positions described above. Personality does play a part. Some individuals will reach leadership status more frequently than others; they may emerge as leaders in a variety of different settings. Others do so rarely or not at all. Still others may acquire leadership in certain situations and not in others. Whether they do or not will depend on whether they have followers. This may sound like a tautology, but it involves the important implication that leadership cannot be understood without taking into account on the one hand the nature of the group concerned and the situation in which leadership is exercised, and on the other the character of those whom the group is prepared to follow.

This middle-of-the-road position appears to be supported by the available research evidence. The effect of the nature of the leader and of the specific role he assumes emerges clearly from an important study of experimentally created "social climates" (Lewin *et al.,* 1939). A number of boys' clubs were constituted in such a manner that the members of each club had approximately the same range of social and personal characteristics; they were then given three different kinds of leaders: authoritarian, democratic, and laissez faire. In the authoritarian setting, the "dictator" made all the decisions; in the democratic situation, policies were agreed upon by group discussion; under laissez faire there was complete freedom, the leader supplying information when requested to do so, but taking no part in the discussions. Since the same individuals took turns in assuming these three different leadership roles, their own personality characteristics may be regarded as having been subordinated to the *type* of leadership involved. The results showed that there was much more aggression in the authoritarian social climate, often directed against a scapegoat, a weaker member of the group who could not easily defend himself. When the authoritarian leader left the room, work almost invariably stopped, whereas in the absence of the democratic leader the group would usually continue what it was doing. The large majority of boys preferred the democratic over the authoritarian setting; results for the laissez faire climate were not so definite. It seems clear that this study may be regarded as having demonstrated the effect of the nature of leadership on the behavior and attitudes of the groups concerned.

Conversely, a study by Merei (1949) shows us the other side of the same coin. In children's play groups, certain youngsters emerged as leaders, who tended to be the initiators of new activities, and whom the other children usually followed. These leaders were then removed from their groups and kept busy in other ways; the remaining children continued with their play, and in a short time developed certain new "culture patterns," new ways of organizing and conducting their activities. When the former leaders were reintroduced into the groups they had previously led, they had to adapt themselves to the new patterns that had in the meantime developed. They could again become leaders only by "following" the rest of their group.

This compromise position that leaders must both follow and lead, seems to apply equally well to the political situation. The explanation of the Nazi movement has on the one hand been sought in the personality of Hitler as shaped by his early failures and resentments, his contacts with Jews, and his Oedipal reactions to his family situation (Bychowski, 1948). On the other hand, a complete account of Hitler's rise to power in Germany must include a description of the forces shaping German attitudes and opinions, and not only the forces shaping Hitler. Erich Fromm (1941), for example, delves into the history of the German people, the effects upon them of the inflation and other economic difficulties through which they had recently passed, the influence of the Lutheran religion, the resentments over the Versailles treaty, and so on. These and other factors seem to him to explain the emergence among many Germans of a "sado-masochistic" character, which predisposed them to accept a hierarchic system in which one owed allegiance to those higher up in the scale of authority and demanded strict obedience and discipline from those below. These same factors help to understand their desire to "escape from freedom," to grant to others (in this case Hitler and the Nazi party) the right to make decisions for the whole people, who were thereby relieved of the painful task of making decisions themselves. To take another example, Erikson (1942) explains the attraction that Hitler had for many Germans because of the similarity between their mentality and that of the adolescent in revolt against parental authority. Without going into the merits of these particular accounts of a specific historical phenomenon, it seems clear that the rise of a leader to power must be understood not only in terms of his characteristics, but also in relation to the psychological readiness of the people to accept that variety of leadership. This point of view emerges clearly in Gilbert's analysis of "The Psychology of Dictatorship" (1950).

It is sometimes argued that, although the people may often exercise a choice or at least a veto in the emergence of a leader, once he has achieved power a dictator can do what he likes without any regard for public opinion. Without denying for a moment the strength that comes from the sheer possession and control of weapons, it is a striking fact that at least in recent times, every dictator has also found it desirable to do everything possible to win the support of the majority of his people. Hitler had a "Ministry of Propaganda and Public Enlightenment" to perform that function, both in order to consolidate his position and, after the war started, to bolster up German morale and the will to win. The frequency with which statements are made "for domestic consumption" in democracies with an eye to the next election, in dictatorships to keep the people in line, also argues for the constant preoccupation with the attitudes of the group as a whole. Dictators may be less sensitive to public opinion, but they cannot be indifferent to it.

Effective leadership is rarely concentrated in the hands of a single individual. Much more frequently the responsibility for major issues in public policy, either domestic or related to the crucial international problems of war and peace, rests with a group of decision-makers who may have varying degrees of influence over the "leader." Members of this group are often referred to collectively as the "elite," not because they are necessarily superior, but because they have power. These are the people to whom the chief of state listens. They do not always come from the same segment of the population, and their composition will vary according to the nation, the period in history, and the specific situations in which they find themselves. They may be the hereditary princes, or the intellectuals, or the leaders of Congress or its equivalent, or the generals, or the "party," or the old men, or as in the case of certain of the new nations, practically everybody with a university education. An understanding of the nature of such elites at any particular time will be just as important as knowledge of the characteristics of the leader on the one hand, or of public opinion on the other.

Frequently, it will be to these elites that the public will look for guidance. As Bonilla (1958) expresses it, "The changing relationship of particular elites to the mass public, as well as the other leadership groups, must be taken into account in any effort to understand the processes of opinion formation in countries where the mass habitually expects and seeks guidance from select leadership groups. It has been suggested that there are significant shifts of the mass from one elite to another with changing political and social conditions."

The special information we need regarding the elite would include the answers to the following questions (Cottrell, 1955): "Who are the élite in a given state and how do they gain and retain their power? Which values are highest in the hierarchy of the élite and which of their values will they sacrifice in order to obtain their higher values? . . . What means are available to carry out the policies of the élite?" Since the decision-makers, though they may be socially and intellectually superior (or occasionally inferior) to the general population, are still part of that population, we must also ask: "What are the prevailing attitudes in the society generally and what is the structure through which it is decided which of these values will be given preference?" Kelman (1955) also speaks of the importance of the shared attitudes that characterize the bulk of the population as well as any segment of it, including the elites. Identifying the values of the elite is in part, therefore, the same process as identifying the values of the society as a whole and involves the application of similar techniques.

The position adopted here, insofar as the attitudes and values held by people are concerned, is that too often in the past attention has been directed exclusively either to the leader or to the general population; that both are important; that a third entity, the decision-makers or the elite, also plays a significant role; that, although their relative weight may vary according to time, place, and situation, there is an interpenetration of the attitudes and values of the leader and the elite and the general public to such an extent that all must be considered simultaneously as an interacting system.

Two further aspects of the problem of leadership require consideration. The first refers to leadership as a *role*. The concept of role, which occupies an important place in the writings of many contemporary social scientists, may be defined as the behavior appropriate to a particular status or position in society; the role of a university professor, for example, consists of those activities and duties he is expected to perform as the result of his occupancy of that particular position. The behavior of any particular individual in that position may be the resultant of a number of interacting factors, including the expectations of society at large, of other professors, of the students, of the president of the university, as well as his own perception of the role as a consequence of his personality characteristics and previous experience. If one's position changes, the new role may be so interpreted as to bring about what may sometimes appear to be a change in personality. Predictions, therefore, as to how a general will react when he is elected president of his country, or a professor when he becomes an ambassador, or a foundation executive when he is appointed Secretary of State, cannot always be safely made. He now has a new "reference group" whose opinions are important to him; his self-image is modified by his conception of what the new role entails. It may very well be that faulty predictions as to how a given individual will conduct himself with regard to foreign affairs are due to excessive concern with what that individual was like previously, and not enough with an understanding of his conception of his new role.

The final aspect of leadership that will be considered at this point is one which has had tremendous international implications. Largely as the result of the devastating impact the Nazi movement had upon the world, considerable attention has been directed toward the phenomenon of pathological leadership, of the assumption of power by persons who are mentally maladjusted. The study by Gilbert to which reference was made above indicates that, while not all of the top Nazi leaders could be diagnosed by psychiatrists as mentally ill, a good many of them could legitimately have been placed in that category. Descriptions of Hitler include many indications of his paranoid tendencies, as well as the fact that he was subject to epileptoid convulsions. It is clear that Rudolf Hess was definitely psychopathic, and the same can be said, to varying degrees, of Streicher, Goering, Himmler, and probably also Goebbels. This means that a substantial segment of the Nazi hierarchy could be so characterized, and that part at least of what the Germans did was due to the fact that they were led by sick men.

Here the writer asks leave to dream a little. Psychiatrists and clinical psychologists are trained to distinguish between normal and maladjusted persons; they make mistakes, of course, but much less frequently than those without such training. If several of them agree in their diagnosis, there is little room for uncertainty. There is therefore available in this area a high degree of technical competence that, if recognized and objectively applied, might have saved the world from the excesses of the Nazi regime, and might also prevent a recurrence of such excesses.

There would have to be agreement that no person could be entrusted with leadership, either in domestic or international affairs, unless he could pass such a test. We have already reached the point, in many countries, of requesting a physician's report on the physical condition of a candidate for public office; we are not as yet prepared to ask for a similar report on his psychological condition.

The reason for this illogical distinction may perhaps be found in the still widespread tendency to surround questions of mental illness and mental health with an aura of superstition and taboo; such issues should not be raised, it just isn't done! This attitude is changing, however, and there is a high degree of probability that in the not too distant future mental illness will be approached with the same objectivity that now prevails with regard to other forms of disease. One can at least conceive of the possibility that some day voters will demand from candidates a clean bill of *mental* health. The necessary examinations could be conducted by a panel of experts set up under national auspices, or with the guidance of such international organizations as the World Health Organization, the World Federation for Mental Health, or the International Union of Scientific Psychology. This suggestion usually elicits a smile on the part of the reader or the listener, and yet such examinations have been required for potential police officers and for employees of such governmental organizations as the United States Information Agency. Is it less logical to demand the same degree of mental health in connection with the higher echelons of public service? The writer realizes that at this particular moment there is no chance that such a procedure will be instituted, but it is legitimate to look ahead to a time when we may be a little more logical in our use and application of available scientific resources. When one realizes that an unstable person in a position of authority may some day be able to press a button that sets a nuclear reaction in motion, the need for such safeguards as have been suggested becomes all the more urgent.

How to recognize mental illness in others may occasionally represent a real problem for a diplomat in a foreign country, where he may be faced with behavior that he finds incomprehensible by the standards with which he is familiar. Since diplomats are rarely trained in psychiatry and anthropology, they may have difficulty in determining whether their lack of comprehension is due to cultural differences in accepted behavior, or to a true neurotic or psychotic condition. In a recent study (Torre, 1962) a list of symptoms that probably have cross-cultural applicability is given for the guidance of the diplomat. These include unexpected and unpredictable emotional responses, extreme swings in mood, generalized hostility, mental impairment, extreme withdrawal from all social relations, compulsive overconformity, and others. Since the symptoms may not always be obvious, the diplomat may frequently find the diagnosis difficult to make with any certainty, but an awareness on his part of the possible range of abnormal behaviors is the first important step in his ability to handle such a delicate situation.

The same investigator presents a frightening account, based on historical material, of the effects of illness, mental or physical or both, on the behavior of persons in a position of leadership, and the consequent influence on the national and international scene. Leaders as different in other ways as President Wilson of the United States, King Ludwig II of Bavaria, and King George III of England, to name a few, all suffered from debilitating illnesses that had serious consequences on a large scale. There is perhaps no need to discuss these findings in great detail; it is, however, important to realize what illness can do to shape the course of events when it strikes people in high places. Our personal sympathy for them must be subordinated to the need for full and adequate information, training in recognizing illness, knowledge of its consequences, and some machinery for keeping sick individuals from wielding power to the detriment of peaceful relations between peoples.

The field of leadership represents therefore another area in which relevant knowledge is available, but one in which the barriers to application are at present almost insurmountable. We turn now to an aspect of international relations in which there appears to be greater readiness to apply the insights of the social sciences. Programs directed toward the technological development of countries and regions in need of aid have in recent years played an increasingly important role in foreign policy and have also constituted a significant part of the activities of intergovernmental organizations. These programs can only be carried out effectively on the basis of an understanding of the traditions and values of the human beings whose lives are being changed as a consequence. It is with this issue that the following chapter is concerned.

7

Changing Men's Lives

*The Golden Rule should be revised to read:
"Do not do unto others as you would they
should do unto you. Their tastes may not
be the same."*

George Bernard Shaw

It is certain that throughout recent history, particularly since the Industrial Revolution, people in many places have been conscious of the rapid pace of social change, and have joined the chorus of "things were very different when I was a boy!" It is also highly probable that a future historian will look back on this particular period of time as characterized by a rate of change which has had no parallel in the past. The liberation of nuclear energy, the ever-increasing speed of communication and transport, the transformation of the political scene through the appearance of many new nations, the spread of automation in industry, and the development of space travel to such an extent as to foreshadow the realization of many of the "extravagant" predictions of science fiction, are perhaps the most striking examples of this acceleration.

For the newer nations, as well as for many areas in the older ones, the rate of change has been most marked in connection with what is usually called technological development. The introduction into tribal or peasant societies of industrial machinery, changes in methods of production and distribution of goods, the use of money as a medium of exchange, the process of urbanization, education along Western lines—all have contributed to a process of transformation of society in one generation comparable to what took place much more slowly and more gradually in the industrialized nations. The transformation has mainly been induced from outside, through programs of technical assistance developed by the wealthier nations through bilateral agreements, through regional groupings such as the Colombo Plan or the Organization of American States, and through the special funds set up for this purpose by the United Nations and its specialized agencies. The assumption is usually made that what we have liked or found useful in our own development will prove to be equally pleasant and palatable to *them*. It is such an assumption that is queried in the quotation from George Bernard Shaw introducing this chapter.

This whole program is frequently described as one designed to bring technical aid to "underdeveloped" nations or regions. This expression has not unnaturally been resented by many of the receiving countries, since the concept of underdevelopment is difficult to keep separate from that of inferiority, and a number of attempts have been made to improve the terminology. The word *"over*developed" has sometimes been applied to the donor nations, evidently on the assumption that if they are criticized for going too far in the technological direction, other nations may not mind being criticized for not having gone far enough. Much more appropriate and accurate is the present tendency to refer to change as a dynamic, continuing process, and to substitute for "underdeveloped" such terms as "developing" or "emerging" to describe those regions receiving technical aid and modifying the nature of their economy as a consequence.

The impulse toward programs of technical assistance is certainly in part ethical and humanitarian, and this motive has undoubtedly influenced many individuals to vote in favor of the necessary budgetary appropriations. There are at least two other motives at work, however, that have, or are believed to have, a bearing on international relations. The first of these is based upon the belief that economic backwardness creates frustration and unhappiness, and that the peoples concerned may be more likely to resort to war as a means of resolving their economic difficulties. Myrdal (1952), for example, speaks of the

> large underdeveloped regions of the world, where huge masses of poverty-stricken, illiterate people eke out an existence of utter frustration and where an immense potential volume of aggression is freely floating and almost *ad libitum* can be directed against the rich, the Jews, the Americans and British or foreigners in general.

(At the same time Myrdal realizes the possibility that internal reform may be "perverted into nationalistic convulsions.") It was probably this theoretical approach that influenced UNESCO to include in its Tensions Project enquiries into "the influence of modern technology upon the attitudes and mutual relationships of peoples." This does not mean that UNESCO regarded the introduction of modern technology as the sole or even the major deterrent against war, since a number of other factors were simultaneously explored. Certainly by itself economic deprivation or underdevelopment explains very little in this context, since modern warfare requires a degree of technical skill and a mass of mechanical equipment that the poorer nations do not possess. In fact a case could be made for the contrary hypothesis, namely, that greater technological capacity increases the ability to wage war, by preparing the way for the harnessing of nuclear energy to military ends. This is why it is anticipated that the "club" of those nations capable of producing atomic bombs will expand its membership in the not too distant future. At the same time UNESCO's concern with this problem has led it to a series of enquiries into the social and human aspects of technological change that have directed attention to certain important implications discussed in greater detail below.

The second motive for technical assistance with international consequences is of course related to the issues of the cold war.

Since both sides want to win friends, to persuade the uncommitted nations to join their ranks, and to keep allies from defecting, expenditures for this purpose may be regarded as an investment calculated to gain additional strength for the struggle. Even when aid is given with no specific strings attached, such a quasi-military or propaganda motive is usually not very far in the background.

Whatever motives, singly or in combination, may be operative, the history of technical assistance programs contains many examples of tragic failures and of maladaptive consequences. Sometimes the allocated funds have fallen into the hands of a few unprincipled individuals, instead of being used for the general welfare; sometimes they have gone to a friendly government, only to have that government replaced by one not so friendly. Methods that have worked well in one country have often been transplanted without change into a new environment where the folkways make them inapplicable; or goods have been introduced without adequate foreknowledge as to how they will be accepted or used. Our values have been assumed to be universal values, which all peoples would gladly accept once they became acquainted with them and were given the means to their realization. Changes have been introduced because they made sense to *us* without adequate consideration as to whether they would necessarily make sense to *them*.

It is unfortunately not very difficult to find examples of such failures. An elaborate and well-equipped school for nurses is set up in a Southeast Asian country but practically no students enroll because nursing is considered a demeaning occupation for respectable young women. Steel axes are introduced into a native Australian tribe and given freely to the women; this causes complete disruption in a community in which axes made of stone had previously been used only by men, for whom they represented the symbols of status and authority. Running water is introduced into the houses in a Greek village but is not used because the women prefer the social contacts that accompany the drawing of water from a communal well, or the washing of clothes in a common stream. The recruitment of young men for factory work in the Congo frees them from the restraints and sanctions imposed by the patriarchal head of the family in the tribal setting, and often develops a disrespect for all authority that gets many of them into difficulties with the law; in other cases the sudden disruption in values and standards may be responsible for an increase in mental abnormality. None of this constitutes an argument against technological change as such. It is bound to occur, and in addition it is now desired and needed in many parts of the world. It has also worked well in many instances and brought much comfort and an improvement in living standards to many peoples. The mistakes that have occurred, however, have been serious, and it is the thesis of the present chapter that most of them could have been avoided by the early application of the knowledge available in psychology and the other related social sciences.

The discipline capable of making the major contribution to an understanding of what hinders and what facilitates change under different social conditions in the developing countries is undoubtedly anthropology, which has as its primary concern the understanding of culture. The specific problems that arise when two different cultures come into contact, with consequent changes in either one or both, have been investigated in many parts of the world, and the attempt to aid in the solution of such problems may be regarded as a fundamental task of applied anthropology. The sad fact remains that anthropologists have usually restricted themselves, or have been restricted, to supplying descriptive accounts of what has happened in situations of change due to culture contact or "acculturation," and have played a relatively minor role in the administrative aspects of the process. It is true, as Beaglehole (1955) points out, that

> various local projects, particularly in the field of public health, have followed the lead of certain colonial and national governments in using the field services of an anthropologist for the day-to-day formulation of policies and the longer range analysis of blockages and resistances that occur in putting policies into practice.

With these few exceptions, however, their contributions so far have consisted mainly in drawing the attention of administrators to the relation between culture patterns and technical change

(Mead *et al.*, 1953), but the logical next step of involving anthropologists in the planning and application of assistance programs has occurred only too rarely.

It should be added that their task under such conditions would not be a simple one, since their research experience has usually been with relatively small tribal units, and the extension of their techniques of interpretation to whole countries may therefore represent a somewhat hazardous undertaking. There can be little doubt, however, that if they had been involved earlier and more directly in technical assistance programs some of the more serious mistakes might have been avoided. One practical suggestion, for example, that has emerged from their research is that difficulties arise not so much from the rate or amount of change as from the unevenness of the process (Mead, 1956). When change is introduced at one point in the culture without adequate regard for the interrelationship of all its parts, the unanticipated consequences may be disastrous.

To the extent that the process of change affects individual human beings, it becomes a psychological problem. This has been recognized by UNESCO, which included psychologists in the research team investigating the effects of industrialization in the former Belgian Congo (Forde *et al.*, 1956). The International Social Science Council conducted a symposium on economic "motivations" in developing countries, and in other ways has concerned itself with the human implications of technological change. It is of course impossible to draw any sharp line of demarcation between psychology and other social sciences. The characteristic feature of psychology is its concern with the individual, but since the personality of every individual is shaped by the group or groups to which he belongs, the psychologist cannot neglect the overwhelming importance of society and culture. There are, however, a number of specific issues in which the psychologist is particularly interested.

The process of radical social change may pose for many individuals, if not for all, a very serious dilemma. Loyalty to one's own community is normally accompanied by pride in its accomplishments, in its values and traditions, in its way of life. Acceptance of change necessarily involves an admission that one's own values will have to be supplanted, or at least supplemented, by others; that somebody else's "way of life" is superior to one's own, either in general or in certain very important aspects. This will frequently create a situation of conflict, which is apparently most marked among those who are in the process of transition from the old culture to the new.

Different individuals, however, even in the same situation, will not react similarly; they will all be affected, but not in the same manner nor to the same degree. Some will accept the changes as not only inevitable but desirable; at the other extreme, change may be experienced as a threat to one's identity or self-concept (World Federation for Mental Health, 1961). In the latter case the conflict may go so far as to induce a real mental disturbance, or a reaction of apathy and despair. Many years ago Boas told of a Kwakiutl chief who lamented the supplanting of the traditional potlatch economy by the more "sensible" system imposed by the Canadian government, and added sorrowfully, "We now have nothing left to live for!" Success in inducing change may well depend on the proportion of people in the community who are truly willing to accept the new culture, and the range of individual variations in this respect may therefore be crucial to planning.

The role of local leadership may also be important in many instances. In the case of the Manus of New Guinea, where changes occurred as the result of occupation by units of the United States Army after World War II, and where the new culture was apparently accepted with very little difficulty, one of the vital factors was the emergence of a gifted local leader who guided the community through the change process (Mead, 1956). The nature of leadership will vary from group to group, and its importance will also vary, since some communities will be more ready than others to "follow the leader." One writer distinguishes between "real" leaders and "status" leaders, and adds a third category of "would-be" leaders, who may be rebels, misfits, or neurotics, and whose activities may sometimes succeed in wrecking a technical assistance project (Beaglehole, op. cit.).

A knowledge of the role of the leaders in the community into which change is being introduced and of their relationship to the followers would seem to be a necessary prerequisite to successful action. There have been many attempts to describe the characteristics of the successful leader under these conditions: as one who has a strong need for achievement, who is willing to take chances, who has the attitude of an entrepreneur (McClelland, 1961); as one who has the quality of "empathy," the capacity to see oneself in the other person's situation (Lerner, 1958). A useful distinction has been drawn between those who initiate change, the "innovators," and those whose example is followed by others, the "influentials." Sometimes these two groups of leaders coincide, but not always, and communities will differ in the pattern of such relationships. It is also helpful to keep in mind the fact that any educational or information campaign designed to change attitudes may operate in what has been called the "two-step" flow of communication. The message may not reach the mass of the people directly, particularly wherever the mass media are limited in their coverage, but it may exercise an effect on those who fill the role of opinion leaders (not always or necessarily those in a position of formal authority), who then transmit the communication to others.

Even if the community and its leaders accept the idea of change, difficulties of adaptation to the new economic situation may arise as the result of certain pre-existing psychological attitudes. Several of these may be mentioned as having particular relevance, although they do not represent a complete list by any means. The first refers to motivation or incentives to work. Even in a complex industrial society many motives play a part; one study revealed, for example, that satisfaction in one's job was determined by such factors as liking the job, work associates, the work itself, the boss, variety, freedom in work, hours of work, and earnings (Hoppock and Spiegler, 1935). Many of these motives may not operate in relatively simpler societies, or they may function in different ways, or they may be secondary and subordinate to other motives (religious, military, and so forth) that take precedence over those related directly to economic enterprise. This does not mean that there are no motives common to all or most men, but their specific character and strength will undoubtedly vary in different societies and individuals. One motive, for example, that appears to play a particularly important role in the developing nations is the desire to be of service to the group or community. This is reported by Biesheuvel in his study of the attitudes of Africans (1959), and was also noted in the "autobiographies of the future" collected by Gillespie and Allport (1955). The African students far exceeded most other groups in their reference to social problems, to the welfare of their ethnic group, and in their emphasis on collective effort and group responsibility. The theme of "self-realization," of being someone, was also mentioned more frequently by African students than by those from other parts of the world. A knowledge of the nature and the relative strength of such motivations would be of great help in presenting technical change in a manner calculated to inspire the maximum cooperation on the part of the people concerned.

A second set of significant attitudes or habits relates to the *rhythm* of work. The human body early becomes conditioned to certain time sequences of varying degrees of definiteness, which divide any given time period into intervals for sleeping and waking, for work and play or relaxation, for intake of food and the satisfaction of other bodily needs, and so on. The move from a folk economy to the behavior involved in working in a factory or any other industrialized enterprise means a fundamental alteration in such deeply ingrained bodily rhythms with consequent difficulties of adaptation; it cannot be easy to learn to "punch a clock" when a man's life has been adjusted to the sun and stars and the sequence of the seasons. It has been suggested that certain features of labor in the developing countries, such as excessive turnover, absenteeism, occasional low production, are partly explained by lack of adjustment to the new work rhythms (Balandier, 1954).

There is in fact a whole set of attitudes related to *time* that are of psychological importance. The suggestion has been made, for example, that an industrialized economy requires an orientation toward the future, toward foregoing present gains for future ones, toward building now for what can be enjoyed only much later. It would be an oversimplification to say that nonindustrialized societies are completely unconcerned with the future; in many instances food may be stored in time of plenty to prepare for later famine. It remains true, however, that people accustomed to a subsistence economy may not be motivated to work longer or harder than necessary to maintain that economy; saving for the future, or building a basis for a subsequent improvement in living standards, may be alien to them. This attitude is illustrated in a story told by Stuart Chase about a kind-hearted employer in Mexico who doubled the salary of the employees on his plantation, with the result that they came to work only every second day. This may be a rare reaction, but the general principle involved, namely, that there are major differences in the willingness to postpone a present gratification for a greater one in the future, or that there may be even a complete lack of concern for the future, appears to be important. There seem to be differences in this respect not only between developed and developing countries, but also between socioeconomic classes in complex cultures, the rule being that the emphasis on the future or the "delayed gratification pattern" is more characteristic of the middle than of the working class (Doob, 1961). Lack of concern for the future has also been pointed out by Italian economists working with peasant groups in Sardinia (Vito, personal communication).

The use of money as a reward for services or as a medium of exchange may also create serious problems of adjustment. As Herskovits (1954) expresses it, "A comprehensive approach must include a consideration of how economic expressions of values are re-ordered into terms of money, where money did not previously exist; or to currency where the tokens used in effecting exchange were not pecuniary ones." Still other problems may result from changes in patterns of interpersonal relations due to movement from a rural to an urban environment; development of a new hierarchy of status and prestige, with the satisfaction and dissatisfaction that this brings to individuals; the formation of new groups and associations resulting from the industrial enterprise, the changing position of women when they join the labor force, and so on.

A brief reference was made above to the effect of technical change on the nature of the family and the individual's place in it. The organization of the patriarchal family, with property controlled by the father or senior male, may create difficulties when a member of the family goes off to work in a factory in the nearest large city. His control over what he earns may be resented; he may be expected to put his money into the common pool, and he may be unwilling to do so; he may seize the opportunity to emancipate himself from parental control, and to loosen the ties binding him to tribal society. Sometimes this may be done successfully, but many cases of personal and social maladjustment and disruption follow such a disintegration of the usual family pattern. These are only some of the phenomena of concern to the psychologist in the transition from a folk economy to industrialization.

Our account of how men's lives have been changed through the introduction of new industrial and economic techniques into tribal societies has painted a gloomy picture of the possible consequences. Similar considerations have led some humanitarians to question the desirability of the whole process and to look back nostalgically to the period when tribal cultures were still pure, whole, and intact. That time has long since passed, however, and whether we like it or not, today the newer nations are seeking help from outside to raise their standard of living, and the more developed nations are prepared, for the various reasons listed, to give it to them. The problem, therefore, is not whether to continue technical assistance, but how. In many cases this has been done successfully, to the great satisfaction of recipients and donors alike. The failures have been sufficiently grave and frequent, however, to emphasize the need to take into account not only the economic, but also the social, cultural, and psychological factors involved in this complicated task; to realize the extent to which "their tastes may be different," and to govern our procedures accordingly. Otherwise, we shall have to answer for more failures.

So far the discussion has concerned itself almost exclusively with the emerging nations. Perhaps the problem is clearest and most acute in their case, but drastic changes in men's lives, as has already been indicated, are occurring in the more developed nations as well. Migration, internal or external, forced or voluntary, may cause a complete disruption in the previous ways of living, disturb the sense of identity, produce a change in status, and create patterns of accommodation and sometimes of hostility with regard to the host community. There are mental health aspects of this kind of change also, although the alleged disproportionate amount of crime among immigrants has never been adequately demonstrated (Sellin, 1937). There is evidence of a slightly greater incidence of mental abnormality, although it is uncertain whether this is due to the stress of change, or to preceding characteristics of the migrants that predispose them to move (Opler, 1960). As far as refugees are concerned, not only is there indication of a substantial mental health problem, but there are also important international repercussions. There can be little doubt that the relations between Israel and the Arab States, between India and Pakistan, between East and West Germany, and between the political East and West in general, have been greatly and adversely affected by the refugee problem. This is of course a political issue with which the psychologist has no special competence to deal, but there are certain aspects relating to the mental adjustment of refugees, the reciprocal relations between them and their "hosts," their emotional ties to their original homeland, their attitudes and expectations regarding a possible future solution for their troubles, all of which are on the one hand psychological in nature, and on the other, have important international implications.

With regard to other changes that are now occurring, little more can be done than to speculate about their future impact. The great development of industrial machinery, leading in recent times to the spread of automation, has changed the character of work so as to remove from it in many cases all feeling of personal accomplishment and "ego-involvement"; work has been "dehumanized" (Friedmann, 1952). Whether this creates the kind of frustration that predisposes the individual to aggressive behavior is, however, problematical. The potential use of nuclear energy for industrial and other peaceful purposes is apparently viewed with a mixture of optimism and fear, and any planning that involves such use should take account of these psychological reactions. An expert committee of the World Health Organization (1959) has pointed out that "It is exceedingly difficult for many people to keep the productive uses of atomic energy clearly separated in their minds from its destructive possibilities and that this inability contributes to making the whole concept of atomic energy potentially a frightening one." Space exploration also has psychological implications, affecting man's picture of the universe and his religious conceptions, widening his scientific horizons and raising the possibility of joint action by all nations in a common, peaceful task. If such a "superordinate goal," common to all mankind, could be used for the purpose of establishing peaceful cooperation between the political East and West in one major undertaking, this would represent an important first step in establishing a pattern of working together that might some day be more widely extended. Agreement has been reached in connection with Antarctica, and there is at least talk of joint activity with regard to exploration in outer space; cooperation in some form and under certain conditions is evidently not impossible (Chapter 14).

This chapter has reviewed some of the facts that have emerged from a psychological and ethnological approach to the human aspects of technological change. It has also stressed the general principle of the need to respect the values and attitudes of those whose lives are being changed; the importance of remembering that "their tastes may not be the same." We turn now to other principles that are perhaps more directly psychological in nature, and that throw light on some of the barriers to international understanding and cooperation. They, too, are based on factual data, but their major function in this context is to facilitate comprehension of ways of thinking unconscious in their origin, and far-reaching in their consequences.

8

Analysis in Depth

Where id was, there shall ego be!

Sigmund Freud

In the preceding discussion, there have been a number of references to the irrational character of many actions and attitudes with relevance to international relations. For a fuller analysis of the nature of this irrationality and the manner in which it functions, we must turn to the theories of Freud. The writer is not a psychoanalyst, nor does he subscribe to all the explanatory principles developed by Freud and his followers. At the same time, it is undoubtedly Freud who has made the greatest contribution to our understanding of personality and has made possible an analysis in depth to which we now turn.

Psychologists will undoubtedly differ in the relative value they would attach to various aspects of Freudian theory. In the writer's view, which he believes would be shared by many others, three contributions are outstanding. The first is the emphasis on the significance of early childhood experience in determining (though not exclusively) the characteristics of the adult personality. The second is the demonstration of the role of the unconscious in motivation. The third and most relevant for our purposes is the identification of various unconscious mechanisms (sometimes called dynamisms) that influence our thought processes. It is to these that we now turn, although the discussion that follows must necessarily be brief and oversimplified (for a fuller critique see Munroe, 1955).

One of the most important of these mechanisms, and the one that is probably most widely known, is *rationalization,* the tendency to interpret our behavior in such a manner as to make it seem just and reasonable. One slightly cynical definition is that it means giving good reasons instead of true ones, since the true reasons are never good, and the good reasons are never true! In a previous context (Chapter 4) it was pointed out how the exclusion of the Chinese from California was justified in terms of their bad qualities ("they deserve it"), and that colonialism was presented (Chapter 3) as an obligation in the form of the white man's burden ("it's good for them"). Hooton (1937) has described this mechanism in graphic if somewhat extreme terms. "Man incessantly seeks to compromise with his conscience or with his innate humanitarianism, by rationalizing his predatory behavior. He must convince himself that the act of grabbing is somehow noble and beautiful, that he can rape in righteousness and murder in magnanimity. He insists upon playing the game, not only with an ace up his sleeve, but with the smug conviction that God has put it there" (p. 151).

Wars are thus presented, with equal "sincerity" by both sides, as having lofty, ethical motives, sanctioned as crusades, as struggles for the liberation of the opposed, as "the will of God." Good reasons can always be found. This does not mean that all wars are equally unjust; the point is rather that whatever their nature or cause, participation in them is almost always seen as due to the best and noblest intentions.

Closely related to the above is the phenomenon of *projection,* which consists essentially in attributing one's feelings and emotions to others. I hate him, but it is wrong to hate, so I project my hatred on to him; it is now he who hates me, and I am therefore justified in taking all possible precautions to defend myself. This is how "preventive" wars may be started; even a little country like Czechoslovakia could be presented by Hitler as a threat to the German nation, so that "appropriate" measures were indicated. It is in this sense that it may be stated there is no such thing as an aggressive war, since from the psychological point of view it is never seen as such by those who start it.

It has frequently been suggested that when things are going badly, when we are unsuccessful and dissatisfied, we are particularly prone to project the blame on someone else; unwilling to take the responsibility for our own failures, we assume that others must have placed us in our present unfortunate position. One of the clearest examples of this mechanism in recent history was the Nazi attempt to blame the Jews for all the troubles that plagued Germany. This was given excellent literary expression in a play by S. N. Behrman, *Rain from Heaven.* One of the characters is a German who has been forced into exile because he wrote a pamphlet called "The Last Jew." He describes its contents in the following words:

> With the extermination of the Jews, the millennium has been promised the people. And with the efficiency of a well-organized machine the purpose is all but accomplished. They are all dead—but one—the last Jew. He is about to commit suicide when an excited deputation from the All-Highest comes to see him. There has been a meeting in the sanctum of the Minister of Propaganda. This expert and clever man has seen that the surviving Jew is the most valuable man in the Kingdom. He points to the Council their dilemma. Let this man die and their policy is bankrupt. They are left naked without an issue, without a programme, without a scapegoat. The Jews gone and still no millennium. They are in a panic—till finally a committee is dispatched—and the last Jew is given a handsome subsidy to propagate. . . .

Jerome Frank, whom we have already quoted, writes: "Many psychological factors go into creating the bogey-man concept of the enemy, such as the convenience of projecting the sources of one's own dissatisfactions and justifying one's own aggressive behavior by use of a scapegoat" (*op. cit.*). It is precisely this mechanism of projection that helps us to understand why frustrated, dissatisfied people are regarded as more likely, other things being equal, to find excuses for starting a war. The historian F. Schuman (1939) emphasizes this explanation for the onset of World War II.

Projection is in turn related to *displacement,* in which a forbidden impulse, such as aggression, is overtly expressed, but against a substitute object. The employee who has had a difficult time with his boss may not be in a position to show hostility against him, but that evening at home he may be especially unpleasant to his wife and children. As has already been noted, a number of writers regard this mechanism as perhaps the major cause of war; due to childhood frustration, aggression against the parents, particularly the father, is stored up until later in life it finds its displaced outlet in violence against a generally accepted enemy. We have rejected this theory as the universal cause of war, but it may function as a contributing factor. A similar phenomenon occurs when leaders present their followers with an out-group as the target of aggression that might otherwise be directed against the leaders themselves.

In a somewhat more indirect manner, it has been suggested that the resentment of a weak nation against a stronger one might also represent a displacement of the original aggression against the father. Farber (1955) writes, for example, that "an unconscious hatred of the father carried over from an unresolved Oedipal conflict may be displaced onto strong authority figures and manifested specifically by a resentment against the United States on the part of a citizen of a weak country." One can only speculate as to the extent to which this mechanism plays a part in determining the greater frequency with which the foreign press, even in friendly countries, reports American difficulties as compared with successes in solving such an important domestic problem as that of race relations.

Still another psychoanalytic mechanism with implications for international relations is *denial,* in which an unpleasant experience is assumed never to have occurred, or a present dangerous situation dismissed as nonexistent. The relative lack of concern

among people all over the world with the devastating consequences of nuclear war is a striking example of this process.
As Frank (*op. cit.*) expresses it, a "common maladaptive response to an overwhelming threat is the denial of its existence."
He goes on to describe other variations of the mechanism of
denial; the belief that nuclear weapons will not be used just
because they are so terrible; a tendency to speak reassuring
words even though they are no longer applicable; an inability
to face up to the dangers of the modern world because of "in-
sensitivity to the remote"; a fallacious appeal to the historical
fact that with the advent of each new weapon alarmists in the
past prophesied that it would destroy mankind, and they were
wrong, and so forth. All of this produces a kind of apathy or
fatalism, which prevents people from making an effort to avoid
the danger simply by denying that it exists.

There are a number of other relevant mechanisms: *repression,*
which is in essence a dismissal from consciousness of unsavory
experiences in our individual or collective past so that only the
more successful episodes are recorded and remembered; *resistance,* which is an unconscious refusal to interpret our reactions
correctly, an unwillingness to recognize the real motives that
activate ourselves or others, in our own or allied nations; *isolation,* related to the phenomenon of logic-tight or watertight com-
partments, enabling us to hold simultaneously two opposed and
contradictory positions; *undoing,* a kind of negative magic, in
which a token act is performed, like giving a piece of land to
an Indian or African tribe, to undo the wrong done to them
when they were driven from their original homes, and the like.
These and other mechanisms, although they have been listed
individually and labeled, are not independent of one another;
they function together. When a nation persuades itself that it
must go to war in self-defense, there may be rationalization to
justify its actions; projection of the aggression onto the enemy;
resistance against accepting the truth, and so on. Collectively,
these mechanisms protect our good impression of ourselves or
our country, and prevent us from seeing ourselves as we really
are (whoever "we" may be).

In Freudian terminology, the original impulses toward thought and action come from the part of the personality known as the *id,* which is the repository of our instinctual drives. The id is under the domination of the pleasure principle, that is, it seeks instinctual gratification and is not subject to the laws of logic, nor to considerations of external reality or expediency. It is the *ego,* which is in contact with the outer world, which has learned how to function in accordance with the reality principle, which can evaluate the external situation, and which modifies the pursuit of pleasure in accordance with that situation. It is the ego that can control the id impulses, and substitute reason for irrationality. This is what Freud had in mind in the statement quoted at the beginning of this chapter. The hope of the world lies in the ego.

Freud has sometimes been called the prophet of the irrational, and an advocate of the free expression of instinctual impulses. Nothing could be further from the truth. He threw light on the irrational, he understood it as no man had before him, but he was its critic, not its advocate. He wanted man to know himself but to control himself, keeping the id subservient to the rational (the ego) and also to some extent to conscience (the superego), which he saw as the judgment of right or wrong, learned from parents and society and incorporated (introjected) into our personality. It is the ego that must take over the complicated task of personality integration. "Where id was, there shall ego be."

One further psychoanalytic mechanism requiring discussion is *identification,* the process by which the son sees himself as one with his father, not only in the sense of copying his speech, his gait, his mannerisms, but often more fundamentally as a "chip off the old block," a part of the same reality and made of the same substance. Similarly, an individual may "identify" with his group, with its leader as a father, and with its members who are all brothers, and sons of the same father. This mechanism can become of fundamental importance in the form of identification with the nation, and therefore in the development of nationalism. As has already been indicated, nationalistic sentiments may have their positive aspects, but the exaggeration of such identification is dangerous. Social controls and sanctions make it impossible to boast, as we might like to, about ourselves or even about our family, but there are no such restrictions with regard to our nation. As Strachey (1959) points out, only a madman says "I am always right," but this may be said, consciously and self-approvingly about one's country. An insult or injury to me as an individual may have to be swallowed, but in the case of the *mother* country or *father*land, it cannot be tolerated. Such an attitude has obvious dangers for international peace, dangers that are increased because, in Strachey's judgment, the attitude involves a regression to a lower level of mentality, and interferes with the use of common sense and reason.

The emphasis throughout this discussion on the need to substitute reason for irrational impulse raises the question as to whether we are dealing here with a problem in mental health. When the World Federation for Mental Health was founded in 1948, a statement was issued with the phrase, "The goal of mental health is to enable people to live together in one world." The words "mental health" in this context are used in a positive, not a negative sense, that is to say, to refer not merely to the absence of mental illness, but to the presence of certain characteristics which, as Jahoda (1958) puts it, improve "the quality of living."

Just what characteristics are important is not easy to determine. Jahoda's survey of the relevant literature identified six different criteria of mental health that have been advocated, all of which have relevance to international relations. (1) The attitudes toward the self, including the accessibility of the self to consciousness, the correctness of the self-concept including the acceptance of the self with its limitations as well as its virtues, and a sense of identity, an awareness of "who and what" one is. This concept is closely related to Freud's "Where id was, there shall ego be," and in its emphasis on the nature of identity, touches also on the question of national identification. (2) Growth, development, self-actualization, including a rich differentiated life, leading to positive feelings for others, for mankind in general. This point has especially obvious implications for international relations. (3) Integration, balance, a unifying outlook on life. It is suggested that such integration is facilitated by a religious outlook which usually includes a conviction of the brotherhood of man, and therefore indirectly, if not directly, a preference for peace over war. (4) Autonomy, independence, the ability to stand on one's own feet and arrive at one's own decisions. Such independence would clearly involve relative freedom from group pressures, and consequently the capacity to resist the more extreme forms of nationalist thinking. (5) A correct perception of reality, free from the distortions due to needs and wishes, and including also sensitivity in the understanding of other people. This criterion is perhaps closest of all to the position presented throughout this discussion. (6) Finally, environmental mastery; adequacy in the interpersonal relations involved in love, work, and play; adaptation and adjustment to situational requirements. This, too, has implications for international relations, since mastery of the environment means adaptation to an interdependent and interconnected world. Even if there is no single acceptable criterion, this analysis does indicate that peace would be greatly facilitated if mental health, however defined, were more widely present. There is certainly no more important task for the specialist in mental health than to help people to live together in one world.

This chapter has leaned heavily on the teachings of psychoanalysis, in spite of the writer's very definite reservations about certain aspects of the Freudian position. The extrapolation from the experience with mental patients to the behavior of whole nations has been questioned, as has also the relative failure of many psychoanalysts to give adequate consideration to social and cultural factors. War is after all an historical institution, accepted by some societies, and not by others, as a legitimate means of settling international disputes; it is not just the reflection of uncontrolled impulses coming from the id. At the same time the attitudes of individuals do play a part, and psychoanalysis is helpful in understanding the irrational nature of such attitudes, and the mechanisms that underlie them. In particular, Freudian theory has clarified the manner in which such mechanisms interfere with an adequate perception of the external world. The next chapter discusses more fully the difficulties in determining the truth about reality.

9

What is Truth?

Vérité en deçà des Pyrénées, erreur au delà.
(*Truth on this side of the Pyrenees,*
error on the other.)

Pascal

It is difficult for most people to realize that their perceptions are not always a faithful and objective image of external reality. Even though everyone knows that a mother usually "sees" in her child qualities not discernible to anyone else, and that a lover finds in his sweetheart a beauty no one else perceives, it is still widely believed that "seeing is believing," and that the evidence of one's own senses is a safe guide to truth. The facts available to the social scientist show that this is by no means always the case, and these facts have important implications for international affairs.

In the first place, we perceive according to our training, our previous experience. An Australian native can follow tracks through the bush, using clues that are simply nonexistent for the untrained observer. The same native would hear the sounds of New York City as a confused blur, unable to distinguish what is due to the automobiles, or to the buses, or to airplanes over-head. The mechanic can detect the slightest irregularity in the sound of a motor; and the trained musician, an infinitesimal devia-tion from the correct tone. Anthropological evidence indicates that odors regarded as pleasant in one community may be dis-agreeable in another, and that there is the same variation in the experience of the consonance or dissonance of tone combinations. On the experimental side it has been demonstrated that familiarity with certain complex words makes them easier to recognize, and that training with optical illusions reduces their effect.

Secondly, we perceive according to our mental set, our ex-pectations. The mother hears the cry of her sick baby when no one else does, and the person awaiting an acquaintance at a street corner "sees" him coming a number of times before he actually appears. Errors in proofreading frequently occur because the reader, especially if he is the author of the manuscript, knows what the words should be and sees them accordingly. The Tro-brianders "see" sons resembling their father, because that is what they expect to see, but they never see brothers looking like each other. An early experiment demonstrated that because of the popular expectation that intelligent people have high foreheads, those who were judged intelligent were also "seen" to have high brows; actual measurement showed no such relationship.

Thirdly, we perceive what we want to. This is the cornerstone of Freud's theory of errors in perception as developed in his *The Psychopathology of Everyday Life,* 1904; such errors are allegedly due to wish fulfillment, though frequently in an indirect and devious fashion. Thus, we may fail to hear a place-name correctly because it reminds us of something unpleasant, or we may "hear" a different name because it is related to someone whom we are anxious to see again. On a more direct level, the influence of wishes was shown in an experiment in which am-biguous drawings were presented to hungry college students, who tended to perceive them as food objects—sandwiches, salads, roasts, and the like. No such effect was found in the case of students who had just finished eating. In another experiment, students were divided according to their dominant value systems (religious, scientific, and so on) and then shown a number of words so quickly that they were at first ambiguous: they were usually seen in a manner congruent with the predominating values. In still another demonstration of the importance of values, it was found that coins were judged to be larger by poor children than by those from richer homes.

When schoolchildren were asked to judge how well some of their classmates performed certain exercises, they usually reported that the ones they liked were superior, even when the opposite was true. Common observation also supports this interpretation; in a baseball game, a close decision at home plate will be "seen" as accurate only if it favors "our" team. Even the most honest tennis players need a referee to ensure that their wishes do not bias their perceptions. In psychological research special precautions must be introduced so that the investigator's desire to verify his hypothesis may not unconsciously cause him to distort his observations in the preferred direction.

In the fourth place, we may alter our perceptions because of the influence of others around us. A whole series of experiments has demonstrated that many subjects will adapt their judgments to those made by others; the distance through which a point of light moves, or the length of a line, may be seen differently as a consequence. The young Crow Indian used to go to the top of a mountain and fast four days, after which he would see a vision of his guardian spirit and hear its voice telling him what occupation he should follow; he had learned from his group that this was what would happen if he carried through the ritual correctly. There is a pressure toward conformity in many if not most of us; we want to be accepted by others, to be "correct" in our perceptions and judgments, and we tend to make our beliefs congruent with those of others in the group to which we belong.

There may be other factors involved, but these are sufficient for our purposes. Obviously they will not act upon all of us all of the time nor to an equal degree. Some observers will be more ready to conform than others, and some will be more prone than others to see what they want to see. The evidence of our senses is certainly trustworthy much of the time. The important point in the present context is the realization of *possible* distortion in our perceptions, and of some of the factors responsible.

All of this in the writer's judgment has serious and important implications for international relations. In the analysis of national stereotypes it was pointed out that they may cause us to select, ignore, distort or reinterpret the perceptual experiences presented to us by the behavior of specific ethnic or national groups (Chapter 4). It is now possible to see that similar phenomena extend over a much wider area, and that no aspect of the international scene is immune to their influence. Because an individual identifies with his own nation, he usually takes it for granted that what his nation does is right, and if those "on the other side of the Pyrenees" disagree, they must necessarily be wrong. He selects and pays attention to those facts that justify this position, ignores those that might presumably point in the opposite direction, and distorts or reinterprets the remainder.

This proposition may give the impression that it has been stated in too extreme terms. The writer of course recognizes that there are many persons who are reasonably objective in their perceptions and judgments, who criticize the acts of their government (although this is relatively easier if they are members of the opposition party), yet who remain loyal and patriotic citizens. For every individual, however, who sincerely says "right *or wrong,* my country," there must be thousands who never question the fact that whatever their country does must be right. This reaction is greatly facilitated by the tendency to divide the world into devils and angels, those who are against us and those on our side, for this is so much easier than trying to distinguish all the intermediate shades.

Usually the whole propaganda machinery of a country is mobilized, particularly in times of crisis, to defend and bolster the official viewpoint, and most people echo what they have read and heard from these sources of "information." The other side of the issue goes by default, or is presented as distortions by the "enemy." Sometimes a circular process may be involved, as when a newspaper or an intelligence agency adopts a policy, sends out men to report on facts pertinent to it, selects the reports and the men that seem most favorable to the policy, and then receives from these men further reports still more favorable, and so on (Deutsch, 1953). Political factors may thus override the need to obtain accurate information; wish-fulfillment replaces objective facts. Some of the failures due to action based on "intelligence" reports may be explained on this basis. It is easier for foreign service officers to send back news that will show they are on the right side, when the alternative is to risk unpopularity and possible failure. In this case it is not always possible to distinguish between what is seen and what is regarded as expedient to see.

One phenomenon that has struck a number of observers of the international scene is the fact that the opinions and attitudes of two contending sides may be mirror images of each other. A psychiatrist writes, "all evidence indicates that the Russian view of the Americans is a mirror image of our view of them; that is, we—or our leaders—are war-mongering, untrustworthy, and dangerous, while they are peace-loving and honorable" (Frank, *op cit.*). A psychologist with an excellent knowledge of the Russian language found it an eye-opening experience to travel through the Soviet Union, to converse with people in many different walks of life and to find them preoccupied and worried by exactly the same fears of us that we have of them (Bronfenbrenner, 1961). A journalist examined a number of our actions, military and political, in various parts of the world and raised the question of how they would look to Ivan Ivanovitch, the average Russian; the evidence was impressive that Ivan's perceptions would not coincide with our own (Snow, 1947). The present writer was in the Soviet Union shortly after the U-2 incident; he found it impossible to convince his Russian acquaintances that our purpose in sending the plane was entirely defensive, due solely to our worries about *their* intentions.

It would be easy to multiply examples. The same external phenomenon, like American aid to Greece and Turkey a few years ago, is seen differently by ourselves and the Russians; we were aiding legitimate governments to defend themselves against rebels; the Russians viewed this as unwarranted interference with the right of the people to otherthrow rulers whom they no longer wanted. The sending of food to a people in need, when "we" do it, is a humanitarian act; when "they" do it, it is using food as a political weapon. Arming the West Germans is considered by most Americans as essential to the defense of Europe; to the Soviets it represents a threat, intensified by their memories of the devastation caused by the German army in World War II. Soviet handling of the Hungarian rebellion appears to us a brutal act of repression; they see it as having been necessary to safeguard their position in Europe. A suggestion coming from one side of the conference table may seem sound and constructive; the same suggestion from the other side is interpreted as an example of Machiavellian double-dealing. This is not always true, of course, but it happens often enough to constitute a real problem (White, 1961).

The concept of the mirror image is helpful and important, but it does not quite tell the whole story. To the extent that the value systems of two nations differ, their perceptions may not necessarily be replicas in reverse of each other. The ideas about the meaning of democracy, for example, are sufficiently at variance so that interference with free elections in a particular country will arouse different reactions no matter who is responsible for it. The present writer has therefore proposed the term "ethnocentric perception" for the phenomenon under discussion. This is related to, but not identical with, *ethnocentrism*, which indicates bias or prejudice in favor of one's own ethnic group. Ethnocentric perception is the tendency to see and judge external occurrences in terms of one's particular ethnic or national identification, that is to say, in terms of the values, wishes and expectations acquired as a member of a particular community. This is what makes it possible for an American and a Russian to look at the same phenomenon and see it so differently.

The material under review has potentially the greatest practical significance for international affairs. Right and wrong become in part a question of where we stand. The problem of the resettlement of Palestinian refugees as perceived by Arabs and Israelis, and the status of Berlin for Americans and Russians are simply different phenomena. One can only guess at how much misunderstanding between nations is due to such group-determined differences in how we perceive. Robert Burns wrote:

O wad some power the giftie gie us
To see oursel's as ithers see us!

This is important, but it is also important to see the world as others see it, or rather to understand how and why others see external reality as they do. Occasionally someone in a position of leadership goes so far as to recognize the existence of ethnocentric perception. Former Prime Minister MacMillan, for instance, has been quoted as saying after a conference with Khrushchev, "We see the world differently." This is at least a first step, but no political leader in the knowledge of this writer has ever taken the indispensable next step of trying to understand why this is so, and progressing to practical conclusions.

One psychologist has suggested that there are three stages in social thinking: "(1) We unconsciously project our own frame of reference onto others; (2) we recognize the relativistic nature of Alter's [that is, the other person or nation] frame of reference but not our own; (3) we realize the equally relativistic nature of our own frame of reference" (Osgood, 1961). This is a difficult position for anyone to achieve, but a recognition of the need to do so should constitute the first essential move in the right direction.

It is not being suggested that ethnocentric perception is the only reason for international disagreements; it may not even be the major one. Even if the external world were seen in the same manner and with equal accuracy by both sides, there might still remain a true conflict of interest or of values that no amount of mutual "understanding" would resolve. The argument here is that the perceptual aspect is an important one, and that if we disregard the manner in which truth changes into error when it crosses the Pyrenees, we fail to take into account a significant human factor in international relations.

One other related concept requires discussion in this connection. As the late American sociologist W. I. Thomas pointed out long ago, what is important in shaping our attitudes and our behavior is not so much the objective situation as the manner in which we perceive and interpret it, our "definition of the situation." This is in keeping with the above discussions, but it implies also that once we have defined the situation and have acted in accordance with it, this may bring about a change even in the external or objective situation itself. Merton (1957) has indicated how important this process may be. If we begin with a false definition of the situation, this may evoke in us a new behavior that makes the originally false conception become true; he refers to this as "the self-fulfilling prophecy." Suppose, for example, that in a small community a rumor is started that the local bank is in difficulties. (We shall have to suppose further that in this particular instance the depositors are not protected by insurance.) The bank may on the contrary be perfectly sound, quite capable of handling all withdrawals to be expected in the ordinary course of events. The rumor spreads, however, and there is a run on the bank, which cannot meet the excessive demand for funds now placed upon it and has to close its doors. The prediction has come true because people acted upon it.

A similar argument has been developed by other social scientists, although the terminology differs. Myrdal (1944) has spoken of a vicious circle in the treatment of American Negroes. They are regarded as inferior; therefore they are treated as inferior, given poorer schools, inadequate housing, fewer economic opportunities; therefore they become inferior, not in the sense that their genes are thereby affected, but in terms of their achievement or standard of living. Those who originally considered the Negro to be inferior can now state with some sincerity (which is never a safe guide to accuracy of judgment) that they were right all the time.

The most direct application of this concept to international relations, and more particularly to war, has been made by Allport (1950), who speaks of the "principle of expectancy." In essence, this means that if we expect a certain event and act accordingly, that event is more likely to occur. The expectancy of war, therefore, increases the likelihood of war. There is nothing mysterious about this principle, if we add the proviso that the acts must be related to the production of the event. If all of us expect rain tomorrow, that will make no difference to the weather, since obviously our behavior is irrelevant to this particular outcome. If, on the other hand, everybody expects stocks to go down and therefore sells out in a hurry, an atmosphere will be created that could certainly contribute to a drop in their value. The late President Roosevelt had a clear conception of this mechanism when he told us that all we had to fear was "fear itself." As far as war is concerned, the expectation that it is definitely coming prevents us from taking all possible measures to avoid it, and therefore makes war that much more probable. The reverse is not necessarily true; war may come when we least expect it. The point is that, if we do expect war, the chances of its occurrence are increased.

If this analysis is sound, it has certain important practical consequences. When our leaders speak and our journalists write of the manner in which World War III will be fought; when a newspaper features "When War Comes to New York"; when we describe Communism as pledged to world conquest by military means; when the Russians, while speaking of peaceful coexistence, describe our leaders as "Fascist warmongers"; when there is so much mistrust on both sides that every act by one is interpreted as aggressive by the other—all of this enhances the probability of war. If we, also on both sides, spoke more of the ways to achieve peace, more of how to strengthen our confidence in the United Nations, more of the fact that a nuclear war is unthinkable, the chances of avoiding it become just that much greater.

There is, however, a distinction which must be made, namely, between expecting that war will come and being prepared if it does come. The line of demarcation is hard to draw, but an analogy may be helpful. Most of us carry fire insurance on our homes. We do not expect our houses to burn down, but we do take precautions against that eventuality. This is not an entirely satisfactory guide to action in the international field, but it may help a little. The writer believes, however, that the suggested program for building shelters as a defense against the effects of radioactive fallout in case of war is both defective and harmful; first, because it can never be so extensive as to take care of the whole population and is therefore discriminatory; second, because it offers only temporary protection, since the effects of radioactivity will remain in the air and on the ground after people have to leave the shelters; third, because it gives a false sense of security; fourth, because it may convince our opponents that we are preparing for hostilities, and may therefore encourage them to strike first; and last (though related to the above) because of its contribution to the expectancy of war. These psychological aspects of the problem should not be ignored in future planning.

It is difficult to escape the influence of ethnocentric factors on our perceptions, or to place ourselves in the position of others so as to understand the nature of their perceptions. The realization of the relativity of what we see and hear is, however, a necessary step on the road to international understanding. *We* may be right, and *they* wrong; the important point is that their definition of the situation is different from ours, determined by a different frame of reference, shaped by other sets of values and presuppositions. Agreement will be possible only when the barrier of ethnocentric perception is overcome (Chapter 14).

We turn now to another variety of potential contribution by psychologists to international affairs. Certain techniques have been developed that have already proved their value at the national level; they have international implications as well. Their use may be expected to make more objective and more reliable many of the judgments that must be made by those who play a role in connection with the relations between nations. Among such techniques, the one that has attracted most attention and has been most widely applied refers to the study and measurement of public opinion.

10

The Man in the Street

Vox populi, vox Dei.

There is a continuing argument as to the role of public opinion in connection with international relations. On the one hand it is suggested that the voice of the people is sovereign and that leaders pay attention to the "man in the street" (one is tempted, however, to ask "what street?"). The Tensions Project of UNESCO accepted this view at least in part, emphasizing the need to investigate the most effective means of changing men's attitudes so as to facilitate peaceful cooperation rather than conflict. The opposing view holds that public opinion is an effect rather than a cause, that it does not create a political climate but reflects it. A sociologist writes:

> The realignment of political powers has had little re-
> lationship to national stereotypes or prejudice or hos-
> tilities or individual attitudes of any kind. The national
> stereotypes and attitudes have followed rather than

preceded the realignment . . . individual tensions seem to follow rather than to precede changes in inter-group relations (Bernard, 1957, p. 54).

We have already encountered this issue in connection with the question of stereotypes (Chapter 4).

As so often happens in controversies of this kind, the truth most probably is to be found somewhere in between. The political situation and the accompanying propaganda campaign succeeded in aligning most Germans behind Hitler in World War II, but the Italians were much less enthusiastic about following Mussolini. The communist regimes in eastern Europe are not equally stable, nor equally certain of the support of their people; pre-existing attitudes, including the prevailing degree of friendliness toward the Western democracies, undoubtedly have an effect. The safest position to adopt is that the relationship is a circular one, with public opinion and the political situation mutually influencing each other. The analysis by a political scientist of the relations between American public opinion and foreign policy argues in favor of this conclusion (Almond, 1950).

Although the relationship is circular, its exact nature will be determined in part by the characteristics of the society, which will affect the amount and kind of influence exerted by public opinion. The national structure may determine the extent of the people's power to influence governmental policy, as well as the opportunity to communicate popular wishes to the decision-makers. It may also "largely determine the actual content of public opinion by affecting the kinds of information that will be communicated to the public. A totalitarian regime, for example, is in a better position to manipulate public opinion since it has almost sole control over the mass media of communication" (Kelman, 1955).

If public opinion needs to be taken into account in the analysis of the international scene, then the question of how to determine with accuracy and certainty the content of such opinion becomes an important one. It is precisely here that the social sciences can be of help through the application of certain techniques designed to make the study and measurement of public opinion as objective and scientific as possible. Although these techniques, and particularly the public opinion polls, have become most widely known as a means of predicting the outcome of elections, they now have a wide application in government and industry and are being used on an increasing scale in a number of different countries.

As far as concerns elections, the outstanding failure occurred in 1948, when the polls pointed to the victory of Dewey over Truman for the presidency of the United States, and it became fashionable to express considerable skepticism regarding all polls as a consequence. As a matter of fact, the proportion of successful predictions has been relatively high, and although the methods used have been severely criticized, often by the practitioners themselves, there can be little doubt that the procedure is on the whole a sound one. At the governmental level, which is of primary relevance to this discussion, it is known that public opinion surveys were made for the late President Roosevelt preceding his fireside chats, so that he knew where the people stood with regard to proposals he wished to present to them; a similar procedure was apparently followed by the former French Premier Pierre Mendès-France. In the United States during the war, opinion surveys were used, for example, in connection with War Bond drives, to discover the motives influencing people to buy bonds, so that such motives might be emphasized more strongly in future selling campaigns. One of the leading experts in this field speaks of the public opinion polls as "the pulse of democracy" (Gallup, 1940), because they are the most effective method, in his judgment, of determining the opinions and the will of the people.

A distinction should be made between public opinion polls and more complex surveys designed to investigate opinions and attitudes. The former usually depend on one or two questions; the latter more frequently involve an extensive interview schedule, which may take an hour or more to complete, and which probes more deeply into the reasons for the answers given. As a consequence they are more informative and dependable, and also considerably more expensive. For present purposes, the polls and the surveys may be discussed together; whether one or the other, or some intermediate form, should be used depends on the purpose of the investigation and the facilities available. Several problems in the application of these techniques have special relevance to international relations.

The first, and possibly the foremost of these, refers to sampling. A foreign-service officer stationed, for example, in Thailand may be expected to report back to Washington on the reaction of the Thais to an American program or proposal. He will send in his appraisal, probably based on the particular Thais with whom he has conversed, and on what he has read in the local newspapers. He has no way of knowing whether his "sample" of informants is representative of the population generally. If he is in a country in which the people are on the whole not in support of the government, his sample may be a biased one, since, as an accredited representative of *his* government, he is more likely to be given the official rather than the popular opinion. He may not have a polling organization or a survey research center at his disposal with which to make up for the defects in his reporting, but he himself can do something to overcome this lack by approximating their techniques as closely as possible. Obtaining a truly representative sample is a complicated statistical procedure, since the group interviewed must be so constituted as to be in miniature a cross section of the population as a whole. Perhaps the best that our hypothetical official could do is to make sure that those whom he does interview come from many different backgrounds—economic, political, educational, regional, religious, and so forth—depending on the variations found within the country. Even this would be an improvement over what is often a haphazard procedure.

The usual polling and survey techniques are similar to democratic elections in the sense that any individual counts as much as any other; one man, one vote. It is useful to draw a distinction between public opinion in general, and what might be termed the *effective* public opinion, the nature of which will undoubtedly vary from country to country. In a pre-election poll in the United States, for example, we would weigh equally the opinions of all potential voters, men and women, urban and rural populations, old and young, rich and poor, educated and relatively uneducated. Depending on the political issue with which we are concerned in a particular country, these subgroups may vary greatly in the influence they exercise. In Brazil, to take one example, successful predictions were made some years ago on the basis of a pre-election poll confined to the large cities; this would be a very dangerous procedure in the United States. One would hazard a guess that at the present time the influence of the relatively few university graduates in certain of the new African states would be completely out of proportion to that of a similar group in most countries of Europe and North America. College students undoubtedly play a more active role in the politics of many Latin American and European nations than they do elsewhere; the role of women also varies greatly.

Considerable knowledge of the social structure of a region is necessary in order to determine just what constitutes the effective public opinion. One psychologist, after indicating the need to obtain information regarding the operation of the communication process, as well as the attitudes and motives of those who receive the communications, emphasizes the importance of the power structure of the society.

> A cabinet minister, a leader of the opposition, a well-known writer, an importer, a commanding general, and a "man in the street" all have different potentialities for action because of their positions in the power structure. We would need information about how decisions are made on economic, political, diplomatic, military, and related matters, the groups in the country which participate in these decisions, and the extent of their participation (Gladstone, 1955).

The special concern with the opinions of leaders or of the elite, as distinct from a representative sample of the general population, would enter into such an analysis.

A second major problem concerns the framing of the questions designed to elicit public opinion; this has been described by one expert as "a nightmare in semantics." There are certainly many pitfalls for the untrained. These include leading questions that begin with "Don't you believe that . . ."; emotionally toned words like "exploitation" or "imperialism" on the one hand, and "democracy" or "freedom" on the other; the use of language that seems perfectly clear to us but that may be ambiguous to our respondents, and so forth. In connection with this last point, a question used by the American Institute of Public Opinion in 1943 read: "After the war, would you like to see many changes or reforms made in the United States, or would you rather have the country remain pretty much the way it was before the war?" When the respondents were questioned more closely, it was discovered that some of them were thinking of domestic changes or reforms, others of changes in the basic politico-economic structure of the United States, and still others of changes in foreign affairs (Crutchfield and Gordon, 1947). Our hypothetical foreign-service officer will not have an easy time.

His difficulties will be increased unless he takes the trouble to learn something about the cultural patterns that prevail regarding the answering of questions. Different peoples will vary in their readiness to be interviewed; in one country strict anonymity will have to be promised and preserved, whereas in another it may be an insult not to ask for the name of one's informant; there are places where truth is subordinated to politeness, which means telling the questioner only what he would like to hear. This list of cultural variations could probably be greatly extended.

The reference to truth touches upon the very important issue as to whether the answers given in a poll or survey really reflect the opinions of the respondents. One study showed that there could be a marked discrepancy between actions and verbally expressed attitudes. An American sociologist traveled through the United States with a young Chinese couple, and everywhere they went and in all the hotels and restaurants they visited, with a single exception, they were treated with courtesy and consideration. When, however, letters were sent to these same establishments asking whether they would be willing to accept Chinese as guests, the overwhelming response was in the negative (La Piere, 1934). In contrast with this finding, however, which may be due to special circumstances, is the fact that pre-election polls usually do have predictive value. In general, people vote as they say they will vote. This constitutes a strong argument in favor of at least moderate reliance on verbal responses as an index of future acts, and therefore of present attitudes and opinions.

This reliance may be increased when more elaborate surveys, rather than polls, are utilized, since there is an opportunity to check the consistency and the meaning of the answers given.

The study of change in public opinion over time may give important information regarding the direction in which a community is going, and may therefore make it possible to make predictions about probable future developments. In the United States, for example, a National Opinion Research Center study in 1956 indicated that only 14 percent of white respondents in the South were willing to accept Negro children into integrated schools. This small percentage acquires significance, however, when it is noted that in 1942 the corresponding figure was only 2 percent. The trend is clear, even though the proportion was still small in 1956. An analysis of public opinion polls in the United States before World War II showed how the attitudes of Americans toward active participation gradually became more favorable as time went on (Cantril, 1944). It has been suggested that repeated surveys should be conducted in many countries, under international auspices, constituting a "tensions barometer," in order to detect at an early stage those tensions that could produce conflict between peoples, so that steps might be taken in time to prevent violence (Dodd, 1950). This idea has so far not been put into operation mainly because there are so many countries with authoritarian regimes that will not permit polling operations, or that control them to such an extent that certain questions just cannot be asked. This is another instance in which the social scientists have a potential contribution to make, but are unable to do so because their competence is not recognized nor accepted.

With regard to trends over time, special attention has been given in recent years to the panel method, in which the same individuals are interviewed repeatedly (Lazarsfeld, 1951). This has the advantage of showing specifically whose opinion has changed or remained constant during the interval, and the interviews may uncover the reasons responsible. This may give a much better basis for predictions regarding future developments, particularly if the "panel" consists of an influential elite whose opinions count in the country as a whole.

Individuals usually share the prevailing opinions of the group to which they belong. Any individual is, however, simultaneously a member of a number of different groups, and these may have opinions which are in conflict. He will then be subject to what has been called *cross pressures* (Berelson *et al.*, 1954). In the United States, for example, Catholics tend to vote Democratic and bankers, Republican; a Catholic banker's vote will therefore be somewhat difficult to predict. An African leader who has been to the University of London may be pulled in one direction by his British education and in another by his resentment against the previous colonial regime. Similar cross pressures may be found in communists who are also Catholics or among some American Negroes who achieve high status in a segregated society, and who are therefore ambivalent toward the trend to desegregation. An understanding of such cross pressures may also be important for the prediction of future behavior.

The group to which an individual belongs—his membership group—is usually also his reference group, that is, the group to which he wishes to belong, or which he uses as a norm or standard against which to evaluate himself or others. Sometimes, however, the reference group may be one to which the individual does not belong, but which serves as a point of reference for his own attitudes and behavior. This phenomenon may frequently be observed in a member of the working class who aspires to be upwardly mobile, and who patterns his behavior in terms of what he considers to be true of the middle class, to which he would like to belong. A Great Power may serve as a positive reference group for a representative of a small nation, who may literally not know what he thinks about a particular issue until he receives the appropriate cue. The U.S.S.R. plays this role for members of the Communist Party in many other countries. There may also be negative reference groups, as when we move away from a position just because it is held by others; the Communists, for example, constitute such a negative reference group for a great many Americans, and vice versa. This is an especially dangerous factor in the formation of public opinion on international issues, since it causes many of us to defend a viewpoint for the sole reason that people we dislike are against it. Finally, reference groups may be imaginary, as when we act in accordance with an erroneous view of what a particular group is like, or what it expects of us. When we decide to "do as the Romans do," our behavior may be determined by the characteristics we ascribe to them, rather than by those they actually possess (Chapter 4).

A further important consideration in assessing public opinion relates to the fact that respondents show a definite tendency to answer questions in the direction of the *status quo*. In a study in the Federal Republic of Germany, for example, the percentage of those favoring capital punishment dropped from 70 to 55 immediately following the abolition of the death penalty. In this case the change was not great enough to bring the majority into line with the new policy, but where opinions are more evenly divided a shift of this size might easily transform a minority into a majority. Before the schools in Washington, D.C., were desegregated, most of those who were interviewed expressed opposition to the admission of Negroes, but after the change had been introduced, more than half reported that it was working well and that they were reasonably satisfied with it. This phenomenon may be particularly important when the attempt is made to measure the effect on public opinion of the introduction of a new policy or program; the amount of change may be due in part to the fact that there is now a new *status quo,* and may not be entirely the consequence of the new program itself.

These considerations are presented as a partial guide to the individual concerned with public opinion; they are far from constituting a blueprint for conducting a poll or survey. The process of obtaining a representative sample of the total population and preparing a suitable questionnaire or interview schedule requires technical knowledge and long experience; the same applies to the training of the interviewers and the recording and analysis of the responses. The diplomat cannot himself be expected to do the job of measuring or appraising public opinion; he needs the experts to help him. He needs also the background against which he can assess critically the information they supply to him. That information, though far from completely dependable, is a definite improvement over any other data available to him, in the shape of letters from correspondents or newspaper editorials or conversations with casual acquaintances.

One specific example of the use of public opinion measurement in an area relevant to international relations may be mentioned as representative of the possible application of this technique. When the Soviet Union successfully launched its first satellite (Sputnik), there was naturally high interest and great concern in the United States regarding the effect of such an achievement on attitudes in allied countries. Surveys conducted in England and France did indeed show that the widespread popular conviction regarding the scientific and technical superiority of the United States had suffered a severe blow, and that this had produced a definite effect on a number of related opinions and attitudes. Before Sputnik, 39.9 percent of the British sample had viewed the West as stronger than the U.S.S.R.; after, the figure declined to 25 percent. Before, 29 percent of the British had wanted their country to be neutral in the Cold War; after, there was a rise to 38 percent; in France during the same period, this rise was from 39 percent to 57 percent (Almond, 1960). Any intelligent observer could have predicted that there would be a change in this direction, but the extent of the change could be measured only by the application of social-science techniques.

When no experts are available, the diplomat may still be able, however, to improve his methods of collecting data, and may become more aware of their limitations. This issue is especially important in connection with the evaluation of programs designed to improve international relations, where it is also possible and desirable, as we shall see in the next chapter, to apply objective and dependable techniques of measurement.

11

Evaluating Programs
for Improving
International Relations

Myself when young did eagerly frequent
Doctor and Saint, and heard great argument
About it and about: and evermore
Came out by the same door wherein I went.

Omar Khayyám, *The Rubáiyát.*

Some years ago at a UNESCO meeting on the subject of international tensions, the discussion turned to those specific activities undertaken for the purpose of improving relations between peoples and, more particularly, to the effectiveness of fellowships or exchange of persons. An Australian expert present volunteered a personal observation. In Australia, he said, the leaders of organizations and activities devoted to strengthening the bonds between members of the British Commonwealth and encouraging friendly attitudes toward the United Kingdom, were all returned Rhodes scholars, who, after spending two years or more at Oxford, came home full of enthusiasm for the mother country. He then added that the leaders of the movement for more complete independence for Australia and withdrawal from the Commonwealth were also all returned Rhodes Scholars. Nothing is proved, of course, by means of an anecdote, based as it is on fallible subjective generalizations, but it does state the problem of evaluation in clear form. What *are* the effects of fellowships abroad? Do they have different effects in different cases? If so, why?

What is true for exchange of persons appears to be equally true for all action programs designed to attain specific goals such as those represented by the United Nations and specialized agencies like UNESCO. Some of these programs have a long history, but there has been a tremendous increase during the past decade in the application of time, energy, men and materials to their development. They are being intensively supported by individual governments as well as by international organizations. In addition to exchange of persons, which includes fellowships for students, provision for visiting professors, visits from specialized groups such as trade union leaders, such programs may also involve technical assistance, information campaigns through publications and radio broadcasts, visits from artists and musicians, and many similar activities. One of the major goals of these programs is to bring the peoples of the world closer together in terms of cooperation and understanding. The faith and hope underlying these programs have recently been tempered, however, by an admixture of skepticism, directed not at the goals but at the methods used to reach them. What in fact has been accomplished? To what extent are we really obtaining the results we have in mind? How good are our methods? How can they be improved so as to achieve maximum effectiveness?

In one sense there has always been "evaluation" of a sort. Program administrators and those who have participated in action projects at various levels have made reports of progress and in some cases of failure, and it is probable that such reports have often been informative and helpful in further planning. Frequently, however, such reports are fragmentary and subjective; they fail to carry conviction precisely because we can never be sure whether another observer, looking at the same project, might not have come to an entirely different conclusion. It is not sufficient to draw attention to the need for evaluation. What is needed is not merely more evaluation, but more acceptable evaluation, based as far as possible on the rigorous demands of scientific method. The goal must be objectivity—of which one criterion is that different experts, using the same techniques, and equally versed in such techniques, will emerge with the same results. To attain that goal requires emphasis on techniques of evaluation.

In this sense—the development of methods of evaluation that should be objective, systematic, and comprehensive—evaluation may be described as relatively new. It is important, therefore, that the term "evaluation" should, as far as possible, be restricted to a process that satisfies such scientific criteria. As such, it should be distinguished from all forms of assessment that take the form of one man's *judgment* of the success or failure of the project, no matter how sensible and wise that judgment appears to be. Although this is perhaps not the place to enter into an argument over definitions, it would certainly be helpful if the term "evaluation" were not used quite so indiscriminately as it has been in the past. It is important to stress precisely this scientific aspect of the process, to consider the need for a base line, from which changes that have occurred may accurately be determined; to stress the importance of a control group, similar in every respect to the group to which the action program has been applied (the experimental group), except for the fact that it has not itself been influenced by such a program. As was already indicated in connection with public opinion, it will often be necessary to examine or interview a representative sample of the population concerned, and to develop methods and techniques that do not depend on unverifiable general impressions; one can be objective even in connection with subjective phenomena such as attitudes and opinions.

Evaluation, therefore, may be described as the process that enables the administrator to describe the results of his program, and thereby to make progressive adjustments in order to reach his goals more effectively. It is important to note that evaluation is not restricted to application at the end of a program, but involves periodic investigation at many stages in the process. In the field of the mass media, a methodology has been developed with extreme sophistication, particularly in connection with the effects of advertising campaigns, to which an extensive body of accepted techniques has already been applied. In other fields the development has proceeded more slowly, but in the work of the social scientists a wide range of techniques is available from which the administrator may make his choice. Many of these have been developed for research purposes, and a major problem in certain fields of evaluation is to discover the means by which these techniques may be adapted to administrative practice, and to the requirements of specific projects. Very often, when the social scientist is asked whether one or another method of carrying out a specific program is more effective, his answer will be: "I don't know, but I can find out."

One of the aspects of evaluation that may appear rather obvious but that still requires some clarification refers to the question of the goals or aims of any particular action project. This is in essence the problem of *values*. In order that the social scientist may be able to give efficient help to the administrator in the development of evaluation techniques, he must have clearly before him the purposes the administrator has in mind in setting up a particular project. If an educational program is introduced into a developing country, the purpose may be to train an elite, or to raise the general level of literacy, or to improve industrial techniques, or to win friends, or any combination of these. It is usually beyond the competence of the social-science consultant to formulate the goals; without such a formulation, however, his aid will be greatly restricted and may possibly be worthless. Something can of course occasionally be done to study the effects of a program without too much concern with goals. If one is asked merely what has happened as a consequence of introducing a new school or a change in diet, it may be possible to give a partial answer. This might be described as the natural history approach to evaluation. More frequently, however, the techniques of evaluation must be adapted to the goals. This means that practitioners must be prepared to supply to their social-science consultants, in the clearest and most direct form, a statement of the general principles under which they are operating, as well as the specific purposes for which the project has been launched. Such a clear formulation has not always been forthcoming.

Evaluation is now "in the air"; it is, in theory at least, accepted by many (if not most) practitioners and administrators as a necessary corrective to the tendency to proceed as uncritically in the future as one has in the past. At the same time, they are usually unwilling to devote any substantial portion of their resources to the process. They ask that the techniques be an integral part of the project and cost little in time or money. This places a great burden on the social scientist, whose techniques sometimes involve extensive interviewing, as well as skilled and therefore expensive personnel. In the face of this difficulty, he might perhaps best proceed on two different levels of complexity.

First, he could describe those evaluation procedures which are of such a simple and practical nature that their introduction and application can be carried out by intelligent field workers without any special training in the social sciences. If a questionnaire is to be used, for example, the social scientist can help in formulating the questions so that they are relatively free of ambiguity and not too difficult to answer; he may in that case leave it to the administrator to apply the questionnaire. If reports are to be sent back to headquarters from the field, the social scientist may contribute advice regarding their contents, in order to ensure the collection of data relevant to the evaluation process. In such cases, evaluation may be established as an integral part of the ongoing activity. It is not easy to introduce the technology of the social scientist at the applied level of administrative practice, but at least an attempt should be made to bridge this gap.

On the other hand, where such simple and inexpensive procedures do not apply, the social scientist can show what may be done if adequate resources are available. This task is just as important as the other. It is unfair to raise false hopes of satisfactory evaluation without cost, when the situation does not warrant it—as, for example, when detailed interviews must be held with a representative sample of a fairly large population. This simply cannot be accomplished with little or no money; short cuts are not always available. The administrator might ask himself whether, in the long run, his whole budget might not be more wisely expended if each year a certain small percentage were set aside for evaluation, even if one or more specific projects might have to be dropped as a consequence. It is true that during the first or second year he might accomplish less, but it is probable that later on he might actually do a great deal more, because his decisions as to the most valuable activities would be based on definite evidence. This is a difficult decision for an administrator, who is under a natural compulsion to get as much done *now* as he can; it is, however, a decision which the social scientist would strongly advocate.

Evaluation must, as far as possible, encompass effects that are both direct and indirect, immediate and delayed, local and general. The task is not an easy one, but its importance is so great as to place upon both the practitioner and the social scientist the urgent responsibility of uniting their techniques and their experience in this complex field.

In both national and international programs designed to help the developing nations or to improve relations between peoples, important beginnings have been made in the direction of evaluating the effectiveness of such programs. UNESCO, in cooperation with the International Social Science Council, has published a volume on evaluation techniques (UNESCO, 1955) and engaged in the evaluation of some of its own projects, including its exchange-of-persons program; it has also commissioned the preparation of a book describing practical and specific techniques in the evaluation of technical assistance or "development projects" (Hayes, 1959). This last publication indicates the kinds of changes that are strategic in this connection: (1) changes in individuals, their information, skills, and attitudes; (2) changes in social relationships and institutions; (3) changes in "social overhead capital," which refers to the nature and amount of investment in education, public health, public administration, and so on. It then goes on to discuss the various steps in the evaluation process, beginning with a description of the development project, and a statement of its goals; then a decision as to the kinds of data required to indicate the results of the project, and the manner in which these data are to be obtained; then the collection of the desired data, before, during, and after completion of the project; and lastly, analysis and interpretation of the findings, and a discussion of their implications with those persons who are most vitally concerned in it. The final conclusion as to the value of the project may have to be delayed for some time, in some cases several years, in order to determine how permanent and how widespread have been its effects.

Evidence of the complexity of the evaluation process emerges clearly from a thorough review of what is known and what is still doubtful in connection with the effects on foreign students of a period of training in the United States (Lesser and Peter, 1957). It is pointed out that, during the early postwar period, the casual assumption was made "that any international educational exchange would almost automatically produce desirable results." Later "it was recognized that this assumption was too optimistic and that the wrong kind of training may do more harm than good" (p. 164). It was found that many visitors who came for technical or academic training returned home with anti-American attitudes confirmed or even intensified. It is the recognition of facts such as these that has focused attention on the need for research and evaluation.

The authors of this report draw attention to a number of different factors that may affect the success of the programs. Even before the arrival of the visitors, there is the problem of selection; the necessity to consider intellectual ability, aptitude, age, personality, and motivation of the applicant; his status and degree of responsibility at home; his attitude toward his own nation; the degree of cultural disparity between the host country and his own; his language facility; the orientation he has received regarding what to expect, and the amount of time he will require to reach his educational goals. After he arrives, he usually goes through a "spectator" stage, in which he "is simply observing the new sights and experiences which come his way, and having an exciting adventure" (p. 180). He then enters a second phase, that of "involvement," during which many problems may arise, and a number of disappointments may be experienced. This period can be one of disillusionment and even of depression but it is one through which many visitors must pass. It is usually followed by a third phase, in which the visitor "comes to terms with himself, the United States, and the training experience" (p.181). Then comes the predeparture phase, in which thought is given to the problem of readjustment at home. The usual pattern of experience has therefore been described as a U-shaped curve; a relatively happy spectator phase, then a trough in the curve as the visitor becomes involved, and as he gradually comes to terms with his problems; then again a high point as he succeeds in the process and prepares for his departure.

On the basis of their review of the relevant research and practical experience, the authors make a number of specific recommendations, emphasizing the special importance of the out-of-school environment, such as the possibility of visiting an American home on an easy, informal basis; the desirability of providing some training for the trainers themselves; putting the instruction on a basis of mutuality, with Americans learning from their guests as well as vice versa. The authors conclude by urging the need for further study and evaluation. They state, for example, that relatively little knowledge has been systematically gathered about programs now in operation, and that only a meager beginning at evaluation has thus far been made.

A special problem arises in the case of nationals from Africa or Asia who come to this country, whether as diplomatic representatives or university students, and who have unfortunate experiences with color prejudice. This issue has caused great concern to many Americans in governmental circles as well as elsewhere, especially when incidents of discrimination—in housing, restaurants and hotels, private clubs, and the like—are reported in connection with foreign ambassadors or members of official delegations, and in several cases formal apologies have had to be offered by the State Department or by the governors of the states involved. The coverage of such incidents in the mass media has been extensive, but one cannot help wondering about the frequency of similar occurrences in the case of university students and other visitors who do not have the official status to make their experiences newsworthy. In this connection the present writer will not soon forget his sense of shock, when on a recent visit to Paris, one of his colleagues there, a non-American known for his friendship for the United States, spoke of plans to hold a conference of African students and added: "I don't want to have such a conference in the United States because African students always leave with anti-American attitudes after their experiences there."

This is undoubtedly an exaggeration, but to what extent? In this connection, psychologists could make an important contribution by devoting some of their energy to discovering just what effect a sojourn in an American university has on African and Asian students. The number of such students continues to grow; the investment, in funds supplied by governmental and private agencies, as well as in time and energy on the part of educators and administrators, is very great, but we know too little about the effect of this extensive program. Such studies should reveal also the nature and frequency of unpleasant experiences, the sources of annoyance and irritation, as well as the areas of enjoyment and satisfaction, and offer guidance to those who are seeking to bring about some improvement in the over-all situation.

In connection with the whole problem of the effect of personal contact on intergroup or international relations, the former naive view that "the more contact the better" has been replaced by the more sophisticated position that the *kind* of contact is crucial. It is unlikely that even years of contact between a European overseer and African workers will effect much change in his attitude toward them as long as the status hierarchy remains the same. One discussion of this problem formulates the essential question as: "What kinds of contact under what conditions have what effects on what aspects of intergroup attitudes?" (Cook and Selltiz, 1955). Different contact situations, for example, will not give the same opportunities for the participants to get to know one another, or to accept one another as equals. For this reason it has been suggested that, for contact to be effective in improving relations between individuals or groups, it must be *equal status* contact. This conclusion has been supported by investigations of the effect on whites of membership in the same military units as Negroes, or residence in the same apartment houses. Experiences of this nature may affect not only the specific situation in which the contact has occurred but other situations as well. In the United States, for example, nationwide polls indicate that a substantial majority of the white adult population prefers residential segregation. Among people who have either worked with Negroes or who have had some experience with them as neighbors, there is still a majority that expresses such preference, but its size is considerably reduced. Among those who have had *both* these experiences, the proportion is still further reduced to about half (Jahoda, 1960).

As has already been indicated (Chapter 5) a second important factor facilitating the improvement of relations under conditions of contact is found in those cases in which the two groups concerned depend upon one another, when the aims of both can best be attained through cooperation. This was true of the military units mentioned above, and to a degree also in the housing study. Sherif *et al* (1961), in their careful experimental investigation of patterns of behavior in a boys' camp, demonstrated the manner in which common or "superordinate" goals could resolve tensions and create a friendly atmosphere. The question is still unresolved, however, as to whether the same effect would occur with other groups or individuals, and under different conditions. More research and more program evaluation are needed.

Similar problems arise with regard to the use of information as a means of improving the attitudes of peoples toward one another. "The Voice of America" and its counterpart in many other nations, the publications of the United States Information Agency, the UNESCO Major Project on the Mutual Appreciation of Eastern and Western Cultural Values, and many similar activities, proceed on the assumption that information does have a positive effect on attitudes. This assumption has been questioned; one social scientist speaks of "psychological barriers to communication" (Katz, 1947), and others have written on "why information campaigns fail" (Hyman and Sheatsley, 1947). On the other hand, the sociologist Arnold Rose (1947) has analyzed the results of eleven studies on the effect of school or college courses dealing with intergroup relations; in six of these the change was in the expected direction, in four there was no change, and in the remaining one the results were ambiguous. This survey gives no basis for complete pessimism regarding the influence of information, but it does indicate the need to study the effects of any particular information program before pouring into it all of our resources and energy.

The whole area of evaluation potentially represents a fruitful and practical psychological application to the field of international relations. There are at least three major difficulties and sources of frustration in the way of a satisfactory realization of such a program. The first, to which reference was made above, is that, although the operators (those who are responsible for action programs either as administrators or field representatives) want evaluation, they want it without having to spend any money or use any large part of the time of their personnel. They ask that evaluation be "built in," absorbed in the regular reporting process, without sacrificing any of the on-going operations. This desire is understandable, but it is most frustrating to those who know something of the complexity of the task, and the need for time, money, and trained personnel in order to accomplish it success-fully. The attempt is being made by social scientists to indicate what can be done simply and inexpensively, although at the same time they urge that whenever possible and whenever neces-sary a thorough and more elaborate evaluation program be under-taken. The feeling of frustration persists, however.

A second difficulty, and one that pervades many of the activ-ities described above, consists in the failure of social scientists to communicate adequately to administrators. Few psychologists are successful in writing in language anyone outside their own discipline can understand and apply. The problem is wider, how-ever, than that of avoiding technical terminology. It involves also the need to place oneself at the starting point and within the frames of reference of those who are responsible for action programs. This may sometimes be done through the collabora-tion of people from both sides of this particular curtain. Some-times it requires a closer acquaintance with (and more direct involvement in) the program itself before deciding how it should be evaluated. This is occasionally described as "getting your hands dirty," a phrase that unfortunately may sound just a little condescending. In any case, too few psychologists have taken this time-consuming but frequently necessary method of making themselves more useful.

A third difficulty arises out of the danger that, once the need for evaluation has been recognized, too much may be expected of the evaluator. The task is sometimes exceedingly complicated, for instance, when a government asks to have an evaluation of its whole national program of fundamental education, and care must be taken not to oversell the available techniques. On the whole, psychologists have been careful in their claims, but it may be that this attitude has not always been made as clear as it should be. It was suggested at a recent meeting that they should make their modesty more blatant.

Even modesty may be exaggerated, however, and the social scientist has the right and the obligation to insist that the evaluation techniques at his disposal could improve the quality of action programs designed to promote international relations. There is little doubt in the writer's mind that exchange of persons across national lines and the increase of factual information, are valuable tools in the service of international understanding. They can, however, be made more valuable than they are at present, by more careful consideration of the factors involved.

There is at least one further area of international activity in which the techniques of the psychologist may be practically and usefully applied. In connection with the evaluation of exchange-of-persons programs, reference was made to the problem of *selection* of students as a primary factor to be considered. The selection of suitable personnel, however, is of much wider significance. It applies to many different forms of overseas assignments, including the diplomatic service, participation in technical assistance missions, membership in the secretariat of an international agency, and many other activities in which the choice of the right person for the job may mean the difference between success and failure, or between improvement and retrogression in international relations. The next chapter discusses some of the issues relevant to the selection process.

12

Assignment Overseas

Fa sempre piu bello all' altra riva del fiume.
(It is always nicer on the other bank of
the river.)

Italian Proverb

It is difficult to estimate the extent to which people leave their homeland for distant parts simply because they like the prospect of having new experiences and meeting different kinds of people. This is true for most tourists who, however, return after a short time to the comfort and security of their own firesides. The situation is different for those who go overseas for longer periods, as representatives of their government, as members of international secretariats, or as employees of large industrial or financial enterprises. In their case a number of other factors may play a part, including a sense of duty, a desire to be of service to the international community, economic advancement, or possibly lack of adjustment to conditions at home. This raises the general issue of the motivation for seeking positions abroad, and therefore of the personality characteristics of the people involved. Since there have been frequent reports to the effect that failures in overseas assignments are due much more frequently to personality difficulties than to technical incompetence, the importance of personality assessment in advance of such assignment is clear and unmistakable.

Although a number of different personality characteristics are relevant in this connection, it may be taken for granted that ethnocentrism, or prejudice against ethnic groups other than one's own, is hardly conducive to success in a foreign assignment. Feelings of superiority over the natives of the country in which one is stationed, resulting either in unwillingness to associate with them on equal terms, or in condescending behavior that reveals a belief in their inferiority, necessarily breed resentment and lack of cooperation. Since there is ample evidence that an ethnocentric attitude constitutes a formidable barrier to success in any mission, it becomes of great importance to select for foreign assignments only those individuals who, as far as can be judged, are reasonably free from prejudice.

The problem then becomes one of how to make such a judgment with accuracy and certainty. The existence of prejudice cannot be ascertained with direct questions, since no one who is applying for a foreign mission is likely to admit that he dislikes the people to whom he is hoping to be assigned. The problem in selection thus becomes one of determining by what *indirect* procedures such an important aspect of the candidate's character can best be determined.

One preliminary point may be made that should be obvious, but that has not as yet received adequate consideration. An application is usually supported by letters of recommendation received from acquaintances who are asked to describe the applicant's qualifications and personal characteristics. If such acquaintances know the applicant well, they should also know something about his prejudices, how he feels about other people. Instructions as to the content of letters of recommendation should therefore include a request for information regarding this aspect of the candidate's qualifications.

Earlier it was pointed out (Chapter 5) that prejudice tends to be generalized, that hostility against certain ethnic groups is highly correlated with hostility against other groups as well. To the extent that this correlation holds, it means that, even if the applicant is careful of what he says about the people to whom he is hoping to go, he may still reveal his general attitude when he is asked about *other* groups. He may claim to like people X, but if he is very hostile toward people Y and Z, he may be diagnosed with a high degree of probability as a prejudiced person.

Perhaps the most significant development in this whole field is represented by the discovery that one may with some success predict the existence of ethnocentrism in an individual without asking him any questions whatever about his attitudes toward ethnic groups. Individuals with a great deal of prejudice tend to display consistent differences in personality from those with very little. In the studies that constitute *The Authoritarian Personality* (Adorno *et al.*, 1950) it was found that prejudice is related to authoritarianism; as has already been indicated, the individual in this category tends to be a supreme conformist, he sees the world as menacing and unfriendly, he is a loyal camp follower as long as the leader remains strong, he is rigid and shows limited imagination; he is herd-minded, exalting his own group and dis-liking many out-groups; he is a "phony conservative," waving the flag, but showing many antidemocratic tendencies; he is a moral purist. Often these individuals are on the surface poised, self-confident, and well-adjusted, but fundamentally anxious and insecure; they appear to worship their parents but have strong repressed hostility against them; they blame others for their own faults and misfortunes.

The psychological instrument on which many of these con-clusions are based is the F Scale, which was designed not only to measure authoritarian or "fascist" tendencies, but also to serve as an indirect measure of ethnocentrism. Although the scale is undoubtedly useful for these purposes, certain limitations in its application must be kept in mind. Individuals who are relatively uneducated, for example, or who are low in economic status, are more likely to obtain high scores (to show more authoritarian-ism) than those who might be described as having a greater degree of social sophistication. Older persons tend to have higher scores than younger ones. There are also national differences, with significantly higher scores obtained by German and Lebanese students than by those in the United States (Christie and Cook, *op. cit.*). These facts indicate that, in interpreting the score obtained by any individual, a knowledge of his social and cultural background is also necessary.

There has been considerable discussion of the relation between prejudice and psychopathology. Although we do not have sufficient evidence to speak with certainty on this point, it appears probable that extremely high ratings on the authoritarianism-ethnocentrism complex are indicative of psychological disturbance. One investigator arrives at the following reasonable conclusion:

> It seems likely that the relationship between mental ill-health and authoritarianism does not hold in both directions. In other words while it may be possible to have any degree of mental illness without showing authoritarian attitudes, it may not be possible to manifest an extreme degree of authoritarianism without being psychologically maladjusted (Jensen, 1957, p. 303).

It will obviously be difficult to get applicants, especially those of high status, to fill out the questions in the F Scale. It is suggested, however, that a skillful personnel officer or other interviewer should be able to turn the conversation into channels indicated by the scale, and by keeping a record of the comments made, arrive at a judgment of the position of the individual relevant to the present issue. It should be possible to include some of these same topics in the instructions given to those requested to send letters of appraisal or recommendation. These data by themselves would not justify any dogmatic conclusions regarding relevant personality characteristics, but taken together with other sources of information they may be exceedingly useful.

One investigator (Allport, 1954), in discussing this general problem, stresses the relation between the ability to get along well with other ethnic groups, and a factor called empathy, by which he means "the ability to size up people," "social intelligence," "social sensitivity," or in German, *Menschenkenntnis*. He describes a study in which a number of foreign students in a training school in the United States were asked to name those

Americans from among their fellow students who they thought would be most likely to succeed, and to be accepted, if they entered the U.S. Foreign Service, in the foreign student's home country. He comments as follows on the results:

> The crucial factor turned out to be "empathic ability." Those who were chosen were students who had demonstrable ability to put themselves in other people's shoes; they had skill in sizing up other people; they were sensitive to the other's frame of mind; they were *Menschenkenner*. The unchosen lacked this social sensitivity. Two findings in this research are particularly important. (1) Skill in human relations is not specific to a given culture; all the nations represented chose the same gifted persons. (2) The giftedness consists largely in empathic ability, a flexible capacity to know the other person's state of mind, and adapt to it.

The fact that this empathic ability turns out to be inversely related to the authoritarian syndrome (high score on the F Scale) again indicates that we are dealing with a rather well unified aspect of personality.

The ability to put oneself in another's place, to see a situation as he would see it, represents a valuable indication of the applicant's chances of success with a different ethnic group. This does not always or necessarily mean the acceptance of the other's point of view, but it does involve understanding it and the motives and values it implies. The rigid, inflexible individual, who holds on to his own frame of reference at all costs, is usually incapable of making a successful adaptation to the new social environment. Psychologists have not yet devised any good measure of empathic ability, although it should not be too difficult to do so. In the meantime, relevant information could in part be obtained from acquaintances of the applicant, or through a detailed interview in which the conversation is directed into appropriate channels.

These various factors may all be regarded as related to the mental health of the applicant, and for such a diagnosis there is no substitute for a detailed examination by a psychiatrist supplemented by a series of relevant psychological tests. This was the procedure followed by the United States Information Agency, which has reported a consequent reduction in the number of failures among its personnel. Very recently, however, Congress is said to have eliminated, as an economy measure, the funds needed for this aspect of the agency's program. This strikes the present writer as false economy indeed.

The question of selection procedures for overseas personnel is an involved one, since different tasks and situations require different qualities; the choice of a chief for a technical assistance mission in a developing country, and that of a stenographer for an embassy in a West European capital, can obviously not be made with the same techniques. Further complications arise as a consequence of the fact that the applicant's wife and children must also come to terms with the new environment, and failure of his mission may be due to their difficulties rather than his own. There is good evidence that the wife's inability to adjust is one of the most common causes of such failure, and it is not surprising that the personnel officers of a number of organizations ask for an interview with the wife before acting on the husband's application for employment. Selection procedures related to personality will not be considered with much favor in those instances in which it is difficult to find even one person who is technically qualified for the post and willing to go. Also, as in the case of evaluation of programs, most organizations would like the best of selection procedures applied with a minimum of time and expense.

It is difficult, however, to find short cuts to effective selection. Psychiatrists and psychologists can be of help in determining the personal characteristics likely to contribute to success in a particular position, the kinds of information needed, and the possible sources of such information, the assessment of its reliability, the conduct of the interviews with the applicant and his wife, and the administration of the appropriate tests. Here, too, the psychologist does not necessarily know, but he can find out. Here, too, his contribution is in the direction of reducing waste and increasing efficiency (Torre, 1963).

A factor that cuts across both selection and training of overseas personnel relates to the knowledge of the language spoken in the host country. Reference was made above to the importance of language skills on the part of foreign students coming to the United States, but it is clear that such skills are equally important for the success of Americans stationed abroad. Too often in the past the attitude has been expressed that this was relatively unimportant, that educated people "over there" would speak English, that there were always interpreters available, that it was a waste of time because one never knew how long he would be stationed in that particular country, and so on. The writer from his own experience can testify to one case, which he can only hope is exceptional, of an American foreign-service officer in Brazil who said he was not going to bother learning Portuguese because "I speak Spanish, and I can get along perfectly well that way." There certainly was no evidence of empathic ability here, since Brazilians are especially sensitive in regard to their language. This man's attitude could only alienate his hosts and reduce friendship for the United States.

Knowledge of the language widens the diplomat's contacts, contributes to his understanding, and adds to his enjoyment of his overseas assignment. It is therefore all the more surprising that this has not usually been considered an important aspect of the selection process. There has been some improvement in this direction, and intensive language training is now more frequently offered to foreign-service personnel before they are sent to their new stations. We apparently still have a long way to go, however, before this aspect of selection and training can be regarded as adequate. According to a recent report, the Soviet Union is far ahead of the United States in its attention to this issue, especially in connection with the more "exotic" languages. Referring to languages such as Swahili, Nepali, Telegu, Annamese, and Amharic, spoken by 86,000,000 people, the report states: "The Soviets have platoons of people trained in all these languages." By contrast with this "immense reservoir of language competence . . . this year only four of our Foreign Service officers are studying Southeast Asian languages" (Burdick and Lederer, 1961). The present writer must add, however, that this "language competence" has not been particularly conspicuous among Soviet citizens whom he has encountered at international conferences.

A special problem arises in the case of members of international secretariats, such as those of the United Nations and its specialized agencies. They are expected to be loyal to their organization, to its goals and its ideals; will this interfere with loyalty to their own nation? There are some superpatriots who would answer this question in the affirmative, and who therefore look upon all such international entities as subversive, preparing the way for a world-state in which national sovereignty is to some degree sacrificed. It is perhaps hardly necessary to comment that the United Nations is an association of independent nations, and that any activity in the direction of a world-state or federalism or world citizenship, in the political sense, is not within its province.

As far as loyalties are concerned, there can be no doubt that a high degree of identification can and frequently does develop among employees of international organizations. On the basis of his own experience with UNESCO, the writer can testify to the satisfaction expressed by an American at the success of a Fundamental Education Project in India, by a Swiss on the opening of a research institute in Brazil, by an Englishman on the completion of an investigation of technological change in Africa. All of these were UNESCO accomplishments, and whatever the nationality of the international civil servants, he was pleased when they went well. There is no reason to believe, however, that his own national identification was thereby diminished, or that he experienced any conflict. On the contrary; as a member of the United Nations Secretariat has expressed it: "Those men who are loyal nationals make the best international civil servants. In their life's development they have learned how to be loyal to the United Nations" (Guetzkow, 1955).

There are two considerations that appear especially pertinent in this connection. The first is that national and international loyalties overlap and in a sense coincide. As Americans, we approve of technical assistance to developing countries, of campaigns against illiteracy, of the eradication of malaria. Our own government supports such programs; there is no difficulty, therefore, in giving our aid and encouragement to similar programs when they are conducted under international auspices. There is surely nothing unpatriotic about wanting peace for our own country, and as a consequence working with the United Nations to obtain peace for the whole world. A number of years ago, a group of former officials of the League of Nations agreed that international loyalty is "not the denationalized loyalty of the man without a country, but . . . the conviction that the highest interests of one's own country are served best by the promotion of security and welfare everywhere" (Guetzkow, *op. cit.*). On this basis one could even argue that loyalty to an international organization is indicative of greater, rather than lesser, national patriotism.

The second consideration refers to Allport's (1954) insistence that there need be no conflict in loyalty to two different groups when one of these includes the other. A warm feeling of identification with one's family does not rule out a similar attitude toward one's city or state, nor does pride in being a Texan interfere with pride in the United States. Similarly, Allport reasons, there is no incompatibility between loyalty to our country and loyalty to the United Nations, or to a world order of which we are a part. This argument appears to be a sound one, and it points to the absence of any real conflict in the loyalties of those whose "assignment overseas" is to serve as employees of international organizations, rather than as representatives of their own government. It also indicates that for all of us, those who stay at home as well as those who work abroad, a sane nationalism implies the need to devote our energies to the establishment of a sane international community.

In connection with the issues raised in this and the two preceding chapters, the description of available techniques has frequently been accompanied by an insistence on the need for further research. Psychologists can help, now; they could help still more if we could fill the gaps in our knowledge on the basis of a greater accumulation of scientific data and principles. There has been an encouraging increase in psychological research related to international affairs, but much more is needed.

In the earlier discussion of stereotypes (Chapter 4) it was suggested that the anecdotal generalizations or "pictures in our heads" regarding national characteristics should be replaced by more objective information. This is an area in which considerable research has already been conducted, but as we shall see in the next chapter, we are only at the beginning of a scientific approach to a difficult and complicated inquiry.

CHAPTER

13

The Character
of Nations

Of all the books that no one can write,
those about nations and national
character are the most impossible.

Jacques Barzun

One can only add that, if such is the case, a very large number
of "impossible" books have been written, for the literature in
this field is extensive, and goes back a long way. Historians at
least since the time of Herodotus, diplomats, journalists, missionaries, and ordinary travelers have all tried their hand at describing the character of a nation. As we have already noted
(Chapter 4), most people seem perfectly willing to describe their
own or other peoples, even though the evidence for such descriptions is usually lacking, or at best inconclusive. Can these stereotypes be corrected, or perhaps replaced by a truer and more
adequate account of the character of nations? Or is such a hope
groundless, and its realization indeed impossible?

There are good reasons for skepticism. In the first place, every
nation is a complex, with variations in behavior and personality
according to social class, occupation, region, or role; it has been

suggested, for example, that in many respects there may be more similarity between the inhabitants of Paris and of New York than between the former and a Breton fisherman or a Basque farmer. There may be a "culture of cities" (Mumford, 1938) that affects personality as much as or more than the culture of a particular nation.

A second difficulty arises from the fact that nations may change, and that the characteristics that appear to be true of a nation may not necessarily last through time. The England of the first Elizabeth certainly seems to have been different from that of Victoria. Kohn (1948) points out that at the beginning of the eighteenth century the English were considered to have inclinations toward revolution and change, whereas the French seemed a most stable and stolid nation; one hundred years later exactly the opposite opinions were held. A similar change took place with regard to the Germans: "One hundred years ago, they were thought a very lovable and most impracticable people, fit for metaphysics and music and poetry but unfit for modern industry and business" (p. 9). This is a far cry from the judgments made of the Germans on the basis of the experience of two World Wars. We know that judgments (or stereotypes) can change even when behavior remains relatively constant, but in the cases cited it looks as if the character of nations may indeed have undergone considerable variation through time.

A third problem relates to the sources of information regarding the character of nations, the means by which the evidence for sound judgments may be obtained. Many methods have been used, and they have all been criticized. We shall review these in some detail later, but two comments regarding methodology may be pertinent at this point. The first is that we need to find ways of obtaining information not subject to the bias of the investigator, or to the political alignments that happen to prevail at a particular moment in history. One American anthropologist, for example (La Barre, 1945), using in part a psychoanalytic approach, attributed to the Japanese certain unpleasantly obsessive and compulsive traits, related to the strict toilet training received in early infancy; none of these was found among the Chinese, who on the contrary were "oral optimists," free of anxiety, friendly, warm, and cooperative. This analysis was made when Americans were allied with the Chinese in war against the Japanese, and one is entitled to wonder whether its author feels quite comfortable about it now that the political picture has changed so radically. In this field, perhaps more than in any other, methods are required that are objective, that can be reproduced and checked by others, and that give sufficiently complete and inclusive results. These considerations lead to our second comment, which is that no one method satisfies these requirements, and that as a consequence a combination of several methods must be used. If the same conclusions emerge from the application of two different techniques, these may be said to "validate" each other, increasing the likelihood that what has been discovered about the character of a particular nation can be accepted as proved. So far this has very rarely been done, which is one reason for insisting that, in spite of the extensive literature on national characteristics, much more research is necessary before we can safely substitute fact for fiction in this complicated area.

At a relatively simple level, however, there is a good deal of information available that may be regarded as constituting a preliminary step in the direction of understanding national characteristics. The customs or folkways of a people are not too difficult to ascertain, and this knowledge may help us to avoid unnecessary *faux pas,* and contribute to a more accurate interpretation of the behavior we encounter. This is the thesis of an entertaining book on *Savoir-vivre International* (Daninos and Ogrizek, eds., 1950) written primarily for the traveling Frenchman, and designed to acquaint him with what will be considered "good manners" in the countries he may visit.

Examples could easily be multiplied of the errors and misunderstandings that may arise when such knowledge is not available. In Spain and most of Latin America, if a visitor expresses admiration of a vase or a picture, the host is likely to pick it up immediately and hand it to his guest with such words as: "Take it. It is yours"; the latter may mistake this polite gesture for a genuine gift and go off with the object, much to the chagrin of the unwilling donor. (The present writer was told of several such "social errors" committed by foreigners in Brazil.) Bargaining over price is practically taboo in Britain or in the United States; it is not only permitted but expected in many parts of Europe, Africa, Latin America, and the Middle and Far East. In China, at least before the days of the communist regime, such bargaining over a valuable object might take weeks, during which the participants might gradually develop a lasting friendship. Americans, whose homes are so easily opened to strangers, may resent not being invited to visit a Mexican or a Spaniard with whom they have become friendly, not realizing that the threshold of a house is the most difficult barrier to overcome, and occurs in most cases only at a late and intimate stage of the relationship.

A Frenchman who receives a kiss on the lips from an English or American girl may ascribe to this experience much more seriousness than it deserves, and act accordingly, and erroneously. The ease with which Americans use first names on slight contact may make many foreigners feel that they have been admitted to a close friendship, only to be disillusioned when they discover that nothing more was involved than casual acquaintance. Table manners differ to such an extent that what is taboo in one society is legitimate in another; the East Indian picks up his food with his hand, the Frenchman mops up gravy with his bread, the Swede at a formal dinner party will never *skål* his hostess, the Englishman holds his fork in his left hand and does not keep moving it to the right hand as is customary in the United States. The Brazilian gives his friend a warm and intimate hug, the *abraço,* but looks askance at the French *accolade* in which one man kisses another on both cheeks.

Punctuality is a virtue in Holland but is relatively unimportant in Spain; professional titles are used in Germany much more than in Great Britain; national patriotism is strong in Poland but subordinate to regional or cantonal identification in Switzerland; the Hungarians put their family name before their "first" name, and the Spaniards use a double surname, the first part of which is the name of the father, and therefore the name that should be used in addressing them. The social errors resulting from ignorance of these and similar facts may sometimes be met by nothing more serious than a raised eyebrow or a tolerant smile, but they may on occasion lead to definite misunderstanding and even hostility.

At a slightly more complex level, problems arise out of a misinterpretation of behavior on the part of other peoples, particularly when such behavior is naively assumed to have the same meaning as it has among us. A Japanese will smile when he is amused, but he will also smile on certain other occasions; for example, it is customary for a servant to smile when he is scolded by his master. A smile is the appropriate response under these conditions, and serves the purpose of smoothing over an otherwise unpleasant situation. To a Westerner who employs a Japanese, such a response may be infuriating; he interprets it to mean that the servant is making fun of him. The Japanese servant will also smile when he is forced to report an unfortunate event, for example, the death of his child. This has been interpreted as a polite gesture meaning that the servant does not wish to burden his master with his personal tragedies and therefore smiles in order to indicate to his master that it is not necessary to take the tragedy too seriously; the servant himself can smile at it. This also may be so misinterpreted by Westerners in contact with the Japanese that they see the smile as a sign of cynicism or lack of concern for the most fundamental human relationships. Among the Chinese, it is customary to open the eyes wide as a sign of anger, and to stick out the tongue in surprise. The writer can testify from his own experiences in the Far East how easy it is for such an "emotional language" to be misunderstood. Long ago it was suggested that such errors of interpretation may constitute an important barrier to friendly relations between two nations (Hearn, 1904). In addition to learning the spoken language of a people, one must also learn its motor or gestural methods of communication.

The task of describing the more specifically psychological characteristics of nations is immensely more difficult, but that has not prevented a great many writers from attempting it. One approach took the form of placing national groups within some sort of schematic classification. McDougall (1920) for example, not too surprisingly found his theory of instincts useful for this purpose, and for him racial and national groups differed mainly in the strength of one or another instinct. The French were more *gregarious* than the Germans; the Scandinavian peoples showed more *curiosity* than those of Spain or Italy. Applying also Jung's scheme of classification, McDougall found the nations of northern Europe more introvert, and those of the south predominantly extrovert.

These and similar schemes are not particularly helpful to us. Even the much more elaborate and painstakingly documented system of Oswald Spengler (1926) with its contrast of historical and ahistorical, and also of Faustian and Apollonian cultures, has been so severely criticized for its historical inaccuracies and its schematic oversimplification, that it may be passed over with this brief mention. It may be noted that Ruth Benedict (1934) who applied somewhat similar categories (Apollonian and Dionysian) with considerable success to American Indian cultures, expressed the conviction that such an approach was not well-adapted to the complex societies represented by contemporary national groups.

Another group of writers may be described as treating national character from a journalistic standpoint. Usually without any special training in the social sciences, they write down what they see, or think they see, frequently adding their own individual, undocumented interpretation. Walter Duranty (1941), for instance, attempting to explain the "confessions" during the Moscow trials, writes as follows:

> The answer to that must be found in the difference between Russians and Western races. . . . When confronted by damning facts which they (the Russians) can't deny they seem to find a last satisfaction in "spilling the beans," a final move toward atonement, a feeling that somehow they can square themselves, not perhaps with their judges, but with their own consciences, by telling all the truth.

Lin Yu-tang (1939) interprets the Chinese character to the Western world, describing it as consisting of mellowness, patience, indifference, old roguery (which is a kind of good-natured nonchalance), pacifism, contentment, humor, and conservatism.

(This description, published in 1939, has a strange ring in the light of the contemporary political situation.)

There is some popular psychology scattered through this and similar material, but no proof. The conclusions represent one man's opinion—usually a well-informed and intelligent man—but largely unsupported by any contributory evidence from other sources. At a much more sophisticated level, but raising some rather similar problems, are the writings of many anthropologists in this field. Incomparably better trained than the group described above, with many more cultures at their call for purposes of comparison, with far greater experience in discerning patterns of relationship, they still present us primarily with one man's judgment, one man's opinion.

Margaret Mead's *And Keep Your Powder Dry,* 1942, is an interesting and stimulating book. American patterns of parent-child relationships, early training, aggressive behavior, criteria of success, and many other aspects of American life are presented with skill and insight. We are told that Americans are in one sense all of the third generation, "our European ancestry tucked away and half-forgotten, the recent steps in our wanderings over America immortalized and over-emphasized." We are told also that Americans fight best when the other fellow starts the fight, when the other fellow has more breaks at the start, when we feel that we are on the side of the Right. Unlike the Englishman, who supposedly fights best with his back to the wall, we must have at least some victories to give us encouragement. Americans, we are told further, start life "with a tremendous impetus toward success." Even parental love is conditioned upon successful achievement by the child.

The specific theses of *And Keep Your Powder Dry* seem to require two further kinds of verification. The first relates to their applicability to the American population as a *whole.* Are they true of all classes and occupations, or, to put the question more generally, what is their distribution? Secondly, how much more are they American than, for example, British or Chinese or Austrian? Miss Mead mentions, as an American characteristic, the need to by-pass one's father by choosing another skill than his. Alfred Adler thought this was a widespread phenomenon, particularly if the father was at all successful. Miss Mead ascribes to the peculiarly American situation in which the child's only anchors are his parents (presumably because the young married couple goes off on its own) the frequency of the adoption fantasy, the belief that one is "nobly born" and adopted by one's "parents," when things go the least bit wrong. Is this typically American? Otto Rank, in his *Myth of the Birth of the Hero*, 1914, regarded the adoption fantasy as universal. Miss Mead may be right on both of these, as well as on other counts. We need more data—data that can be collected and that can give a reasonable degree of certainty to what must otherwise remain hypothetical.

Similar questions must be raised about other global descriptions of national psychology. Among the best known of these is Ruth Benedict's *The Chrysanthemum and the Sword*, 1946, which deals with a number of aspects of Japanese life considered to be of major importance, such as taking one's "proper station" in life, the significance of shame as a sanction for good behavior, repaying the "debts" or obligations owed to parents, to the emperor, and so forth. This book, ably and even brilliantly written, has aroused considerable controversy, because other specialists on Japan, including many Japanese, have not always been willing to accept Benedict's data with her interpretation of them. There is in fact a book by Jean Stoetzel, which in its English translation is entitled *Without the Chrysanthemum or the Sword*, 1955, and which, on the basis of public opinion research and attitude studies, raises some important questions regarding Benedict's conclusions, and also indicates some of the changes in "national characteristics" that have occurred as a consequence of the war and the American occupation.

To cite just one more example, the English anthropologist Gorer (1949), with the collaboration of the psychoanalyst Rickman, has attempted an analysis of the character of the Great Russians, using as a clue the tight swaddling imposed by Russian parents on infants during the first year of life. Since the behaviorist John B. Watson pointed out many years ago that restriction of movement caused rage in infants, Gorer finds in the tight swaddling an explanation of the outbursts of violence and aggression he regards as characteristic of Russians. The feeling of guilt accompanying the impulse to aggression may also explain their readiness to "confess" to crimes that as a matter of fact they have not committed.

The present writer finds these attempts stimulating and suggestive, but unconvincing. The conclusions reached, and the data by which they are allegedly supported, are too dependent on one person's opinion. What is needed in the whole area is factual evidence, gathered through techniques that satisfy the criteria of scientific objectivity, that will permit and justify the integrative synthesis of the kind sought by the cultural anthropologist. We are still far from having such evidence to any satisfactory extent, but important beginnings have been made in that direction.

We know, for example, that there is considerably more suicide, year after year, in Austria than in Ireland; Denmark has proportionately more suicides than the U.S., but much fewer homicides. These are facts, though their explanation still remains somewhat obscure. There is fairly good evidence to the effect that schizophrenia, a disease characterized by withdrawal from external reality, is considerably rarer in India than in Western Europe, possibly because the Hindu religion offers opportunities for such withdrawal without resort to what has been called "a flight into the disease." It has also been reported that depression much more rarely accompanies psychoses among African Negroes than anywhere in the Western world.

In addition to these vital and social statistics, data have been obtained through interviews of individuals, along the lines used by psychiatrists or clinical psychologists; the study of attitudes or opinions; the application of personality inventories and projective techniques, including the Rorschach and the Thematic Apperception Test; content analysis of cultural products such as plays or movies; detailed study of individual communities such as Middletown in the United States and Tepoztlan in Mexico. This listing constitutes only a very incomplete summary of the extensive research that has been conducted on national characteristics (Duijker and Frijda, 1961; Klineberg, 1950).

A somewhat closer look at one or two of these studies will give us the opportunity to consider certain additional issues with important practical implications. During World War II it was to be expected that a great deal of attention should be paid to the psychological characteristics of the Germans. One of the qualities most commonly attributed to them was that they were too disciplined, too ready to accept authority, either of the father or of the state, obediently and unquestioningly. In order to check this view, at least in part, the psychologist McGranahan (1946) asked a number of questions of boys of high school age in the United States and Germany. One of these was: "Is a boy justified in running away from home if his father is cruel or brutal?" Sixty-eight percent of the Americans and only 45 percent of the Germans said "yes"; 30 percent of the Americans and 50 percent of the Germans said "no." In general, therefore, the "stereotype" or the common belief was substantiated, but it is clear that there were a great many exceptions; 30 percent of the Americans answered in the "German" direction, and 45 percent of the Germans in the "American." Similar results were obtained with the other questions; there are differences, but they are never of the all-or-none variety. They can best be expressed in quantitative terms, that is to say, in terms of the greater *probability* that Germans will behave in one way and Americans in another, never in terms of *certainty*. This has the important practical consequence of imposing caution in connection with predictions regarding any individual German, and of reducing the tendency to put all Germans in the same psychological category. Even when all the facts are in, we shall still have to avoid statements about *the* Germans or *the* Russians.

A study by Gillespie and Allport (1955) made use of the technique of asking young people to write an "autobiography of the future," an account of what they thought their life would be like until the year 2000. One of the interesting findings was to the effect that in the more recently independent countries (like Egypt) or among groups striving for better status (like South African Bantus) many of the subjects wrote of their plans to be of service to their group or community; in other nations the autobiographies were much more egocentric and self-centered. If this difference is a real one, it appears to be due to the state of national development of the groups concerned, and is probably not a lasting attribute of the people.

Similarly, when the same technique was used in Trinidad, it was found that, in general, the *lower* the actual social and economic level of the subjects, the *higher* were their aspirations for the future (Zavalloni, 1960). Here again, the obtained data may not be related to national characteristics as such, but rather to temporary social position or status.

Although we have by no means exhausted the complexities and difficulties in this area, enough has perhaps been said to indicate that the truly *scientific* study of national characteristics is still in its infancy. It is true that some convergence is beginning to appear in the observed results. In the study of American motion pictures as well as in the autobiographies of young people, the striking fact emerges that, when Americans talk about their family, they mean the family they themselves have produced or expect to produce, rather than that from which they have come; the "family of procreation" rather than "the family of orientation"; this is in contrast, for example, with what happens in English movies or autobiographies. The French, in public opinion studies as well as in the autobiographies, show a considerable degree of pessimism and concern about the future, as contrasted with the prevailing American tendency toward optimism and the belief that anything or everything is possible. These are crumbs of information compared with what we need, but they do represent a first step toward the process of using various techniques to validate and corroborate one another, in a field in which no one technique is in itself sufficient.

Until we have more such data and further convergence, a cautious skepticism must be maintained with regard to any conclusion about the psychological characteristics of nations. Even when we have the data, however, generalizations with regard to all the members of a particular nation will continue to be dangerous and misleading. We may find differences in "mode" or average or central tendency, but there will always be overlapping. In this field, certainty is a chimera; the most that we can anticipate is a greater or lesser degree of probability.

One final word in this connection. A concern with the psychological differences between nations should not blind us to the fact that in many respects all peoples are alike. There are indeed differences, but it is important also to recognize the essential unity of all mankind. In one sense, it is the overemphasis on differences—physical, cultural, ideological—that may be regarded as responsible, at least in part, for conflicts and disagreements between nations. *They* are bad, inferior and wrong; *we* are good, superior and right. Under these circumstances, what if anything can be done to facilitate agreement and make cooperation more likely? Much recent research has been directed toward this fundamentally important question, the topic of our next chapter.

14

The Meeting of Minds

It's the same old stuff; nothing new or constructive in it.

> Almost any American commentator
> on a Soviet proposal.
> Almost any Soviet commentator on
> an American proposal.

If war is to be avoided, there must be at least to some extent a meeting of minds, a readiness to agree on alternative solutions to critical problems, a willingness to negotiate. Much of what has been presented in this book may be interpreted, however, as negative in character, in the sense that it has emphasized the difficulties and barriers in the way of successful negotiations. The conviction of the superiority of one's own group and one's own position: the tendency to polarize, to stereotype, to see differences in terms of devils and angels; the readiness to hate, and to love, irrationally; projecting one's own aggression onto the adversary; seeing the world from one's own ethnocentric viewpoint; these and many other mechanisms may appear to make agreement impossible.

Yet agreements have occurred. History is rich in its record of war, but it is rich also in its record of wars avoided and disputes settled through negotiation. Even the Cold War protagonists have agreed through the United Nations on a Universal Declaration of Human Rights, on a program of technical assistance to economically underdeveloped regions, and on the peaceful use of outer space. The World Health Organization's fight against disease and UNESCO's campaign against illiteracy have both won support from all sides. This does not mean that agreement on more specifically political problems is inevitable or even likely in the near future; what it does mean is that under certain conditions a meeting of minds can and does occur. The crucial question is how to create such conditions with regard to those critical issues which keep the threat of war constantly with us.

There is of course no easy answer to this question. The complex power struggle with all its ramifications, the historical background of national animosities, the competition for markets, join with the psychological factors of mutual fear and suspicion to create the paradoxical situation in which most of the people of the world want a peace, which they do not know how to establish or maintain. Although most men hate war, for many of them there are hatreds even more intense, so that "better dead than Red" becomes an accurate description of the attitude of many people who have convinced themselves that this is the alternative they face. For still others, the failure to reach any agreement with the adversary and the prospect of continuing to live under a thermonuclear threat, may lead to a "let's get it over with" attitude coupled with a fatalistic acceptance of the accompanying destruction. The opposite extreme of pacifism and the Gandhian techniques of non-violent resistance that have on the whole worked well in connection with intergroup relations in this country, so far have affected a relatively small minority, and cannot be counted on as yet to exert much influence on the international scene. The major hope seems to lie in a new approach to negotiation, a new concept of what can be done around the international conference table.

Such an approach, if it could be realized, would have the following characteristics. First, it would be more flexible; the rigidity shown in the composite comment that introduced this chapter and that inhibits any receptivity to fresh ideas or proposals results in the freezing of positions at the status quo. Second, it would be more understanding; it would take into account how the situation appears to both sides, how *our* actions (whoever *we* may be) look to *them,* how our suggestions will be interpreted by those who see the world from a different perspective. Third, it would be less suspicious of the motives of others, and more willing to take a chance on the possibility that a sincere desire for peace is not the monopoly of one side. Fourth, it would be less greedy; it must approach the conference table not with the insistence that "our" side has to win, but with the readiness to find a solution that is reasonably satisfactory to both sides.

The writer is not so naive as to believe that these changes in attitude, reasonable though they may seem to him and to many others, will be immediately recognized as reasonable by those who represent their nations at international conferences. Such representatives, from whatever nation they may come, are much more likely to insist that they themselves are indeed flexible and objective; it is the others who are rigid and ethnocentric. The mirror image in international relations is to a large extent a reality, but one that both parties to a conflict have great difficulty in recognizing. What the psychologist can do is to describe the reality in the hope that insight and information may represent the first step, as they occasionally have done, in modifying attitudes in a constructive direction.

He can do more than that, however; he can apply his technical competence and his research skills in an attempt to discover what is involved in the two types of negotiation, the old and the new, and to indicate some possible ways by which the transition from one to the other may be facilitated. There have been some significant experimental approaches to these problems; in certain cases it has been possible to isolate factors in the conference situation and study them under controlled laboratory conditions. Granting that such an approach will always be subject to the query as to how successfully we may extrapolate from the laboratory to real life, we may safely assume that additional insight will be gained. It may be helpful to keep in mind the fact that in other scientific fields, such as biology, significant research can be carried on *in vitro* as well as *in vivo*.

In one such study, for example, Mouton and Blake (1962)

brought two individuals together with instructions to find jointly the best possible solution to a specific practical problem. These "conferences" took place, however, under two differing conditions. In the first, the participants came together as individuals, with no previous commitments. In the second, the "conference" followed a discussion of the problem in two separate groups, each of which agreed on the solution, and then sent one of its members to meet with the representative of the other group to work out a solution acceptable to both. The solutions were graded for their quality by the participants. The results showed that in the second situation, in which the participants functioned as representatives of groups, with an answer already prepared, they were much more rigid and uncompromising in their positions, and unwilling to change, so that deadlocks commonly occurred. In addition, they were usually unable to judge the quality of the solutions objectively. Clearly, rigid adherence to prior commitments is not the best preparation for finding adequate solutions to difficult problems, even though *some degree* of such commitment may be inevitable at the international level.

The second feature of the new approach to negotiations refers to the need to emerge from the strait jacket of ethnocentric perception, and attempt to see the world as others see it. Here there is an extensive, relevant research literature, based partly on sociometry and partly on group dynamics, dealing with the situation in which one party to a conflict "takes the role of the other," that is to say, puts himself in his opponent's place and makes the best possible case for that side of the argument. The added understanding that results from this experience often has the therapeutic effect of reducing the hostility between individuals. In a field more closely allied to our present concerns, Lippitt (1949) has found that it may also exercise a favorable influence on the relations between Negroes and whites, giving them an understanding of the grievances as well as the values on the other side, and facilitating cooperation and agreement. Anatol Rapoport (1962) suggests that in a controversy each side should be required to state the opponent's position to the latter's complete satisfaction before advocating his own; this would eliminate at least those aspects of the conflict based on misunderstanding. Such a technique has never been tried in connection with international disputes, and it is too much to hope that this will happen in the foreseeable future. Without going through this procedure, however, it may still be possible to approximate its effects by realizing the necessity of understanding the position of one's opponents. As was pointed out earlier, MacMillan said after a conversation with Khrushchev, "We see the world differently." Statesmen who realize this should then ask a few pertinent questions. How? At what point? To what extent? Why? With what consequences? This surely would be more constructive than the naive assumption that *we* see the world correctly, and that *they* do not (Cohen, 1951).

The third proposed change, from mutual fear and suspicion to at least a modicum of trust, is perhaps the most important of all; it is certainly the most difficult to achieve. Not only is there no simple formula for the removal of fear, but the task is further complicated by the fact that so many people on both sides are firmly convinced that the fear is amply justified. Under such circumstances the suggestion that trust should replace suspicion must usually fall on deaf ears.

It is, however, a fact well-known to psychologists and psychiatrists that fear—in animals, in children, in normal and abnormal adults—may easily give rise to aggression. Many years ago the Dutch psychiatrist van Loon (1927) explained one of the most violent of all aggressive phenomena, the act of *running amok* among the Indonesians, as due to the conviction on the part of the sufferer that he is about to be attacked by others; he slashes about in fury to protect himself from his imaginary enemies. Although this mechanism will not operate so directly at the international level, the principle remains the same. Fear of a potential opponent results in the build-up of armaments to deter him from attacking; the opponent does the same. Both sides feel impelled to have the stronger striking power, which they see as a deterrent against aggression by the "enemy." The vicious spiral of fear and armaments continues, with the constant danger that someone in authority will feel that the only way out is to press the button first.

The psychologist has no blueprint for the process of initiating a new pattern of negotiation built on trust. He has two proposals to make which may, however, facilitate that process. The first is to build upon and extend the concept, previously discussed, of common or superordinate goals, shown by Sherif and his co-workers (1961) to have the effect of reducing tensions in the microcosm of a boys' camp, and potentially applicable on the wider international scene. In essence this means cooperation on both sides, together with those who are not identified with either side, in activities of concern to all, and for the purpose of reaching goals desired by all.

In this spirit, for example, the psychologist Morton Deutsch (1962) has advocated a reorientation of foreign policy with the initiation of cooperative trade policies, research programs, cultural exchanges, agricultural projects, and so forth. "Our objective should be simply to promote the values of economic well-being, educational attainment, scientific and industrial development which we share in common and which we believe are necessary to a stable, peaceful world." As has already been indicated, a small start in this direction has been made, but this approach needs to be magnified and multiplied in order to reinforce a pattern of cooperation rather than that of seeing everything, or almost everything, in competitive terms.

The anthropologist Margaret Mead (1961) has expressed a somewhat related view. "The big issue now is the survival of mankind. The time is coming when we will have to be responsible for the Russians' children and they will have to be responsible for ours." This might be phrased a little differently, if less strikingly, in the present context. We and the Russians and all the other peoples of the world have a common interest in children; a superordinate goal on which the whole world can cooperate is help to children, everywhere. It is no accident that the international agency in which political conflicts have been reduced to a minimum is *Unicef,* the United Nations' Children's Fund, which speaks to a common concern of all mankind. We need desperately to find more such areas of common concern. Just as fear begets aggression, so cooperation begets trust.

A second proposal made by psychologists for the reduction of fear and suspicion is identified with the name of Charles Osgood (1962); he has called it "Graduated Reciprocation in Tension-

Reduction: or alternatively "Graduated Unilateral Disengagement." This is seen as a reversal in the arms race, "a deliberate 'peace offensive' designed to induce reciprocation by an enemy." One side (Osgood is making his proposals primarily to the United States) must take the initiative in creating a feeling of confidence and trust in the other through a series of unilateral acts. Such acts, according to Osgood, must satisfy certain conditions. They must be perceived by the opponent as reducing his external threat; accompanied by explicit invitations to reciprocation; executed regardless of prior commitment by the opponent to reciprocate; planned in sequence and continued over considerable periods regardless of reciprocation by an opponent; announced in advance and widely publicized; graduated in risk potential; diverse in nature; not be such as to endanger our "heartland"; accompanied by explicit firmness in all areas.

Osgood goes on to suggest specific criteria for determining those acts to be initiated unilaterally, but these involve considerations that would take us too far afield. He also admits that certain moderate risks are involved. The approach as a whole does give us hope, based on psychologically sound premises, that mutual fears and suspicions may gradually be reduced, and as such deserves careful and sympathetic consideration by policy-makers. As far as the risks are concerned, they appear to be less serious than those accompanying the present impasse.

The fourth feature of the new approach being proposed with regard to international conferences relates to a greater willingness to reach solutions reasonably acceptable to both sides, as opposed to the insistence that our side must win and the other lose. Here, too, there is relevant psychological research that may help to illuminate the situation under discussion. Deutsch (1962) describes an experiment using a two-person game, in which each player has to choose between pressing a red button and a green button. If both press the red, they both lose $1; if both press green, they both make $1; if A presses green and B red, A loses $2 and B gains $2; in the reverse situation, B loses and A gains $2. If they think of their self-interest, the players will both press the red button, on the principle that $2 can be won, and at the most only $1 lost on each trial. If they do so consistently, however, it is clear that they both must lose. "Players oriented toward defeating the other player to their self-interest only, when matched with similarly-orientated players, do in fact choose the red button and do end up by losing consistently." Once again the analogy with the international situation is by no means perfect, but once again the principle is clearly applicable.

This has begun to be realized in high places. In his address at the University of Washington in Seattle in November 1961, the late President Kennedy said,

> It is a test of our national maturity to accept the fact that negotiations are not a contest spelling victory or defeat. They may succeed, they may fail. But they are likely to be successful only if both sides reach an agreement which both regard as preferable to the *status quo,* an agreement in which each side can consider that its own situation has been improved.

One can only express the hope that this attitude will prevail, and that it may in time be recognized by those concerned as a necessary prerequisite to all international negotiations. It is an attitude adapted to political realities, and at the same time consonant with the results of psychological experience and research. If negotiations are approached in terms only of what we can win, and what we can make our opponents lose, the inevitable result is failure. As Milburn (1961) expresses it: "Mutual interpretations of the international relationship as competitive in the sense that only one side can win, may lead to a result where both sides lose."

There will be those who will greet these proposals with righteous wrath and damn them as "appeasement." This raises a series of further considerations related to what Stuart Chase a number of years ago called "The Tyranny of Words" (1938). We are often at the mercy of labels, of expressions used as weapons, their impact sharpened and strengthened by powerful emotions which supercede logic. This phenomenon has already been mentioned in connection with national stereotypes, ethnocentric perception, and the formation of attitudes. Sometimes, as in the case of "appeasement" or "colonialist" in the international area, "egghead" in domestic American politics, "integrationist" in parts of the Deep South, the label itself is sufficient to discredit an individual or a program. In other cases the common procedure is to attach a few descriptive epithets to ensure the "proper" emotional attitude; so we read on the one hand of "atheistic communism," or the "international communist conspiracy," or the "aggressive Eastern bloc," and on the other, of the "imperialistic, war-mongering, Fascist and colonialist" leaders of the West. Some of these descriptions may be truer than others, but their constant use creates an emotional climate that constitutes a major barrier to a meeting of minds.

Another difficulty rarely recognized arises from the need to conduct most international negotiations through translation. Even the best interpreters in the world will occasionally be faced with complex problems of communication. There may be "exact" equivalents for the terms used, but the translation may be misleading if the word has different connotations in the two languages because of varying cultural and historical frames of reference. One thinks here of words like "democracy," "freedom," or "peaceful coexistence," in connection with which translation may be easy but communication difficult.

An example of a slightly different kind is represented by the verb "to compromise," in which difficulties may arise because of differences in the likelihood with which one or another meaning may be attached to it in various languages. As had been pointed out (by Glenn, 1955, for example) the word has two distinct meanings in both English and French, but the first meaning in the one language is secondary in the other, and vice versa. Webster's Universal Dictionary defines it as follows: "1. To adjust and settle (a difference) by mutual agreement, with concession of claims by the parties, to compound. 2. To agree: to accord. 3. To commit; to pledge in some manner or form; *to put to hazard, or endanger (one's character, reputation, etc.) by an action that cannot be revoked*" (italics supplied). The *Petit Larousse* gives as the first meaning of the French *compromettre* (in English translation) *"to expose, to endanger, to embarrass; losing one's reputation, compromising someone."* As a second meaning, it is equated with making a compromise, stipulating that recourse should be had to arbitration. It is easy to understand the unpleasant reaction of a French mind when the suggestion is made "to compromise."

Much more serious in its effect on international relations is the case of the oft-quoted Khrushchev remark, "We will bury you." This has usually been interpreted in its *active* sense, that is, as equivalent to "We will destroy you" or "We will conquer you." The present writer once heard it quoted by an eminent American scientist whose version was "We *are going* to bury you"; and in another instance, it was "We *intend* to bury you." Actually (Bronfenbrenner, personal communication) the translation into "We will bury you" is literally correct, but in the sense that "We will outlive you," or "We will still be alive when you are dead." In other words, it expresses the conviction that Communism will outlast Capitalism, not that the Communists will violently destroy the West. In this case what *appears* to be a correct translation may be very misleading, and aggravate an hostility that is already serious enough.

Language is of course an integral part of a national culture, and problems of communication are intimately involved in the material related to the characteristics of nations (Chapter 13). In the context of international conferences and the accompanying negotiations, cultural factors may play an important part. Margaret Mead (see Capes, 1960) suggests, for example, that such factors may make democratic procedures more palatable to certain national groups, and authoritarian procedures to others; that the committee system, which is Anglo-Saxon in origin, may arouse distrust and hostility among Latins; informality on the part of the chairman may be welcomed by some, and interpreted as disrespect by others; there will be differences in styles of hospitality and courtesy, and so forth. She indicates the need for sensitizing conference participants to the nature of such cultural differences, and finding ways in which members of different cultural groups may actively participate in various stages of conference planning.

Whatever else we may do, however, to make conferences more effective, we must not neglect the problem of the nature of individual participants—not just their cultural background, but their characteristics as individuals. *Selection* (see Chapter 12) thus assumes great importance, in addition to techniques, procedures, understanding of cultural differences, social activities, and all other factors legitimately regarded as playing their part. Since such selection is not always possible, however, the chairman and the secretariat must be constantly aware of the idiosyncratic nature of the individuals who participate; they should have psychological insight, if not psychological or psychiatric training. The extent to which this can be taught has not as yet been established. A challenge is presented by the fact that when we analyse all the possible factors that can be controlled in order to render group procedures more effective, we are still confronted by the x of personality.

To many readers the approach to the meeting of minds described in this chapter is too slowly paced to satisfy a world in search of peace. There is a small but active group that advocates a program of World Federalism, a federation of nations analogous to the federation of American States. Social scientists have also concerned themselves with this possibility. The political scientist Karl Deutsch (1953), for example, has described various problems of definition and measurement of what he calls the "political community" at the international level. The sociologist Robert Angell (1957) states that "One of the great hopes of the world is to discover through social science how to build a more inclusive social system within which States can peacefully cooperate." The present writer has great sympathy with this position, and recognizes that important steps in such a direction have already been taken, although usually in nonpolitical fields. The United Nations, together with its Specialized Agencies, represents the most "inclusive social system" the world has ever known; as such it deserves all the support it can possibly obtain. It is an organization of nations, however, not a federation of states; as such it must operate within the framework of national loyalties and antagonisms that constitute the major barrier to World Federalism. It has therefore seemed more reasonable to the writer as a first step to start from the present situation, and indicate how some of the necessary changes in attitude might be facilitated and a new start in international negotiations initiated. Albert Einstein (1946) put the problem in the following terms:

> Our world is threatened by a crisis whose extent seems to escape those within whose power it is to make major decisions for good or evil. The unleashed power of the atom has changed everything except our ways of thinking. Thus we are drifting toward a catastrophe beyond comparison. We shall require a substantially new manner of thinking if mankind is to survive.

It is in the hope of making a contribution, no matter how modest, to a "new manner of thinking," that this book has been written.

REFERENCES

Adorno, T. W., Frenkel-Brunswik, E., Levinson, D. J., and Sanford, R. N. *The authoritarian personality.* New York: Harper & Row, 1950.

Allen, F. H. Aggression in relation to emotional development. *Proc. Int. Conf. on Child Psychiatry,* 1948, 4–11.

Allport, G. W. *The nature of prejudice.* Cambridge, Mass.: Addison-Wesley, 1954.

———— *Personality and social encounter.* Boston: Beacon Press, 1960.

———— The role of expectancy. In H. Cantril (ed.). *Tensions that cause wars.* Urbana, Ill.: Univ. of Illinois Press, 1950.

———— and Postman, L. *The psychology of rumor.* New York: Holt, Rinehart and Winston, 1947.

Almond, G. *The American people and foreign policy.* New York: Harcourt, 1950.

———— Public opinion and the development of space technology. *Publ. Opin. Quart.,* 1960, *24,* 553–573.

Angell, R. C. Discovering paths to peace. In *The nature of conflict.* Paris: UNESCO, 1957.

Ardrey, F. *African genesis.* New York: Atheneum, 1961.

Aron, R. *Paix et guerre entre les nations.* Paris: Calmann-Lévy, 1962.

Balandier, G. Comparative study of economic motivations and incentives in a traditional and in a modern environment. *Int. soc. sci. Bull.,* 1954, *6,* 372–387.

Baldwin, R. In MacIver, R. M. (ed.). *Discrimination and national welfare.* New York: Harper & Row, 1949.

Barzun, J. *Race: a study in modern superstition.* New York: Harcourt Brace, 1937.

Beaglehole, E. Evaluation techniques for induced technological change. *Int. soc. sci. Bull.,* 1955, *7,* 376–386.

Bender, L. Genesis of hostility in children. *Amer. J. Psychiatry,* 1948–9, *105,* 241–245.

Benedict, R. F. *Patterns of culture.* Boston: Houghton Mifflin, 1934.

———— *The chrysanthemum and the sword: patterns of Japanese culture.* Boston: Houghton Mifflin, 1946.

Berelson, B., Lazarsfeld, P. F., and McPhee, W. N. *Voting.* Chicago: Univ. of Chicago Press, 1954.

———— and Salter, P. J. Majority and minority Americans; an analysis of magazine fiction. *Publ. Opin. Quart.,* 1946, *10,* 168–190.

Berle, A. In MacIver, R. M. (ed.). *Discrimination and national welfare.* New York: Harper & Row, 1949.

Bernard, J. The sociological study of conflict. In *The nature of conflict*. Paris: UNESCO, 1957.

Biesheuvel, S. *Race, culture and personality*. Johannesburg: South African Institute of Race Relations, 1959.

Bird, C. *Social psychology*. New York: Appleton, 1940.

Bonilla, F. Elites and public opinion in areas of high social stratification. *Publ. Opin. Quart.*, 1958, *22*, 349–356.

Brigham, C. C. Intelligence tests of immigrant groups. *Psychol. Rev.*, 1930, *137*, 158–165.

Bronfenbrenner, U. The mirror image in Soviet-American relations. *J. soc. Issues*, 1961, *17*, 45–56.

Bruner, J. S. *Mandate from the people*. New York: Duell, Sloan and Pearce, 1944.

Buchanan, W., and Cantril, H. *How nations see each other*. Urbana: Univ. of Illinois Press, 1953.

Burdick, E., and Lederer, W. J. Big push in Soviet propaganda. *Sat. Eve. Post*, 1961, *234*, 13–15.

Bychowski, C. *Dictators and disciples*. New York: International Universities Press, 1948.

Campbell, A. Factors associated with attitudes toward Jews. In G. E. Swanson, T. M. Newcomb, and E. L. Hartley (eds.). *Readings in social psychology*. New York: Holt, Rinehart and Winston, Inc., rev. ed., 1952.

Cantril, H. (ed.). *Gauging public opinion*. Princeton, N.J.: Princeton University Press, 1940.

Capes, M. (ed.). *Communication or conflict*. London: Tavistock Publications, 1960.

Chase, S. *The tyranny of words*. New York: Harcourt, 1938.

Christiansen, B. *Attitudes toward foreign affairs as a function of personality*. Oslo: Oslo University Press, 1959.

Christie, R., and Cook, P. A guide to published literature relating to the authoritarian personality through 1956. *J. Psychol.*, 1958, *45*, 171–199.

Coelho, G. V. (ed.). Impacts of studying abroad. *J. soc. Issues*, 1962, *18*, No. 1.

Cohen, J. The technique of role-reversal. *Occup. Psychol.*, 1951, *25*, 64–66.

Cook, S. W., and Selltiz, C. Some factors which influence the attitudinal outcomes of personal contact. *Int. soc. sci. Bull.*, 1955, *7*, 51–58.

Cottrell, F. Research to establish the conditions for peace. *J. soc. Issues*, 1955, *11*, 13–20.

Crutchfield, R. S., and Gordon, D. A. Variations in respondents' interpretations of an opinion-poll question. *Int. J. opinion and attitude Res.*, 1947, *1*, No. 3, 1–12.

Daninos, P., and Ogrizek, D. (eds.). *Savoir-vivre international.* Paris: Odé, 1950.

Deutsch, K. *Nationalism and social communication.* New York: Wiley, 1953.

———— *Political community at the international level.* Princeton, N.J.: Princeton University Press, 1953.

Deutsch, M. A psychological basis for peace. In Wright, Q., Evan, W. M., and Deutsch, M. (eds.). *Preventing World War III: some proposals.* New York: Simon and Schuster, 1962.

Dodd, S. C. A verifiable hypothesis of human tensions: an international and basic research for polls. *Int. J. opin. att. Res.,* 1950, *4,* 37–56.

Dollard, J., *et al. Frustration and aggression.* New Haven, Conn.: Yale Univ. Press, 1939.

Doob, L. W. *Becoming more civilized.* New Haven, Conn.: Yale Univ. Press, 1960.

Dorsey, G. A. *Why we behave like human beings.* New York: Harper & Row, 1925.

Dubourg, J. Unpublished Ph.D. Dissertation. New York: Columbia Univ., 1962.

Duijker, H. C. J., and Frijda, N. H. *National character and national stereotypes.* Amsterdam: North-Holland Publishing Co., 1960.

Dunn, L. C. Race and biology. In UNESCO: *Race and science.* New York: Columbia Univ. Press, 1961.

Durbin, E. F. M., and Bowlby, J. *Personal aggressiveness and war.* New York: Columbia Univ. Press, 1939.

Einstein, A. Telegram to *The New York Times,* May 25, 1946.

Erikson, E. H. Hitler's imagery and German youth. *Psychiatry,* 1942, *5,* 475–493.

Farber, M. L. Psychoanalytic hypotheses in the study of war. *J. soc. Issues,* 1955, *11,* 29–35.

Forde, D., *et al. Social implications of industrialization and urbanization in Africa south of the Sahara.* Paris: UNESCO, 1956.

Frank, J. Breaking the thought barrier. *Psychiatry,* 1960, *23,* 245–266.

Freud, S. *Psychopathology of everyday life.* In *The basic writings of Sigmund Freud.* New York: Random House, Inc., 1938. (Translated from *Zur Psychopathologie des Alltagslebens.* Vienna, 1904.)

Friedmann, G. The social consequences of technical progress. *Int. soc. sci. Bull.,* 1952, *4,* 243–260.

Fromm, E. *Escape from freedom.* New York: Holt, Rinehart and Winston, Inc., 1941.

Gallup, G., and Rae, S. F. *The pulse of democracy.* New York: Simon and Schuster, 1940.

Gibb, C. A. Leadership. In G. Lindzey (ed.). *Handbook of social psychology.* Cambridge, Mass.: Addison-Wesley, 1954.

Gilbert, G. M. *The psychology of dictatorship*. New York: Ronald, 1950.

———— Stereotype persistence and change among college students. *J. abnorm. soc. Psychol.*, 1951, 46, 245–254.

Gillespie, J. M., and Allport, G. W. *Youth's outlook on the future*. New York: Doubleday, 1955.

Gladstone, A. J. The possibility of predicting reactions to international events. *J. soc. Issues*, 1955, 11, 21–28.

Goodenough, F. L., and Harris, D. B. Studies in the psychology of children's drawings. *Psychol. Bull.*, 1950, 47, 369–433.

Gorer, G., and Rickman, J. *The people of great Russia: a psychological study*. London: The Cresset Press, 1949.

Guetzkow, H. *Multiple loyalties*. Princeton, N.J.: Princeton Univ. Press, 1955.

———— Isolation and collaboration: a partial theory of international relations. *J. Conflict Resolution*, 1957, 1, 49–68.

Hartley, E. L. *Problems in prejudice*. New York: King's Crown, 1946.

Hayes, S. P., Jr. *Measuring the results of development projects*. Paris: UNESCO, 1959.

Hearn, L. The Japanese smile. In *Glimpses of unfamiliar Japan*. 2 vols., Boston: Houghton Mifflin, 1894.

Hebb, D. O., and Thompson, W. R. The social significance of animal studies. In G. Lindzey (ed.). *Handbook of social psychology*. Cambridge, Mass.: Addison-Wesley, 1954.

Herskovits, M. J. *The myth of the Negro past*. New York: Harper & Row, 1944.

———— Motivation and culture-pattern in technological change. *Int. soc. sci. Bull.*, 1954, 6, 388–400.

Hobhouse, L. T., *et al. The material culture and social institutions of the simpler peoples*. London: Chapman and Hall, 1915.

Hooton, E. A. *Apes, men and morons*. New York: Putnam, 1937.

Hopkins, P. *The psychology of social movements*. London: Allen & Unwin, 1938.

Huxley, J. S., and Haddon, A. C. *We Europeans*. New York: Harper & Row, 1935.

Hyman, H., and Sheatsley, P. B. Some reasons why information campaigns fail. *Publ. Opin. Quart.*, 1947, 11, 412–423.

Jahoda, M. *Current concepts of positive mental health*. New York: Basic Books, 1958.

———— Race relations and mental health. In UNESCO: *Race and science*. New York: Columbia Univ. Press, 1961.

James, H. E. O., and Tenen, C. *The teacher was black*. London: Heinemann, 1953.

Jensen, A. R. Authoritarian attitudes and personality maladjustment. *J. abnorm. soc. Psychol.*, 1957, 54, 303–311.

Katz, D. Psychological barriers to communication. *Ann. Amer. Acad. Polit. Soc. Sci.*, 1947, *250*, 17–25.

———— and Braly, K. W. Racial stereotypes of one hundred college students. *J. abnorm. soc. Psychol.*, 1933, *28*, 280–290.

Kelman, H. C. Societal, attitudinal and structural factors in international relations. *J. soc. Issues*, 1955, *11*, 42–56.

Klineberg, O. *Race differences*. New York: Harper & Row, 1935.

———— Tensions affecting international understanding; a survey of research. *Soc. Sci. Res. Council Bulletin*, No. 62, 1950.

———— Negro-white differences in intelligence test performance. *Amer. Psychologist*, 1963, *18*, 198–203.

Kohn, H. *The idea of nationalism*. New York: Macmillan, 1944.

Kroeber, A. L. *Anthropology*. New York: Harcourt, new ed., 1948.

Kusunoki, K. Mental characteristics of the Japanese race as seen by Japanese and American students. *Japan. J. appl. Psychol.*, 1936, *4*, 232–237.

La Barre, W. Some observations on character structure in the Orient. *Psychiatry*, 1945, *8*, 319–342; 1946, *9*, 215–237, 375–395.

LaPiere, R. T. Attitudes and actions. *Soc. Forces*, 1934, *13*, 230–237.

———— Type-rationalizations of group antipathy. *Soc. Forces*, 1936, *15*, 232–237.

Lazarsfeld, P. F. Panel studies. *Publ. Opin. Quart.*, 1940, *4*, 122–128.

Lerner, D. *The passing of traditional society*. New York: Free Press, 1958.

Lesser, S. O., and Peter, H. W. Training foreign nationals in the United States. In Likert, R., and Hayes, S. P., Jr. (eds.). *Some applications of behavioural research*. Paris: UNESCO, 1957.

Lewin, K. A., Lippitt, R., and White, R. K. Patterns of aggressive behavior in experimentally created 'social climates.' *J. soc. Psychol.*, 1939, *10*, 271–299.

Lippitt, R. *Training in community relations*. New York: Harper & Row, 1949.

Lorenz, K. Z. *King Solomon's ring*. New York: Crowell-Collier, 1952.

McClelland, D. C. *The achieving society*. Princeton, N.J.: Van Nostrand, 1961.

McDougall, W. *The group mind*. New York: Putnam, 1920, rev. ed., 1928.

McGranahan, D. V. A comparison of social attitudes among American and German youth. *J. abnorm. soc. Psychol.*, 1946, *41*, 245–257.

Mead, M. *And keep your powder dry: an anthropologist looks at America*. New York: Morrow, 1948.

———— (ed.). *Cultural patterns and technical change*. Paris: UNESCO, 1953.

—— *New lives for old.* New York: Morrow, 1956.

—— Interview in the *New Yorker* magazine, May 13, 1961.

Mercier, P. Evolution of Senegalese elites. *Int. soc. sci. Bull.,* 1956, *8*, 441–452.

Merei, F. Group leadership and institutionalization. *Human Relations,* 1949, *2*, 23–39.

Merton, R. K. The self-fulfilling prophecy. In *Social theory and social structure.* New York: Free Press, 1949.

Milburn, T. W. The concept of deterrence. *J. soc. Issues,* 1961, *17*, 3–11.

Montagu, M. F. A. *Man's most dangerous myth: the fallacy of race.* New York: Columbia Univ. Press, 1945.

Mouton, J. S., and Blake, R. R. The influence of competitively vested interests on judgments. *J. Conflict Resolution,* 1962, *6*, 149–153.

Mumford, L. *The culture of cities.* New York: Harcourt Brace, 1938.

Munroe, R. L. *Schools of psychoanalytic thought.* New York: Holt, Rinehart and Winston, Inc., 1955.

Murphy, G. (ed.). *Human nature and the enduring peace.* Boston: Houghton Mifflin, 1945.

—— *Personality: a biosocial approach to origins and structure.* New York: Harper & Row, 1947.

—— and Likert, R. *Public opinion and the individual.* New York: Harper & Row, 1938.

Myrdal, G. Psychological impediments to effective international co-operation. *J. soc. Issues,* Supplement Series No. 6, 1952.

—— et al. *An American dilemma.* New York: Harper & Row, 1944.

Nadel, S. F. *The foundations of social anthropology.* London: Cohen and West, 1951.

Nansen, F. *Eskimo life.* London: Longmans Green, 1893.

Nielsen, G. S. (ed.). *Psychology and international affairs: can we contribute?* Copenhagen: Munksgaard, 1962.

Odum, H. W. The errors of sociology. *Soc. Forces,* 1936–37, *15*, 327–342.

Opler, M. K. (ed.). *Culture and mental health.* New York: Macmillan, 1959.

Osgood, C. E. *Alternative to war or surrender.* Urbana, Ill.: Univ. of Ill. Press, 1962.

Pettigrew, T. F. Personality and sociocultural factors in intergroup attitudes; a cross-national comparison, *J. Conflict Resolution,* 1958, *2*, 29–42.

Rank, O. The myth of the birth of the hero. *Nerv. and Ment. Dis. Mono.,* No. 18, 1914.

Rapoport, A. Rules for debate. In Wright, Q., Evan, W. M., and Deutsch, M. *Preventing World War III: some proposals.* New York: Simon and Schuster, 1962.

Razran, G. Ethnic dislikes and stereotypes: a laboratory study. *J. abnorm. soc. Psychol.*, 1950, *45*, 7–27.

Robinson, H. A., and Hoppock, R. Job satisfaction researches. *Occupations*, 1952, *30*, 594–598.

Rose, A. *Studies in reduction of prejudice.* Chicago: Am. Council on Race Rels., 1947; rev., 1948.

Schoenfeld, W. N. An experimental study of some problems relating to stereotypes. *Arch. Psychol.*, 1942, No. 270.

Schuman, F. L. *The Nazi dictatorship.* New York: Knopf, 2nd. ed., 1939.

Scott, W. A. Rationality and non-rationality of international attitudes. *J. Conflict Resolution*, 1958, *2*, 8–16.

Sellin, T. Culture conflict and crime. *Amer. J. Sociol.*, 1938, *44*, 97–103.

Sherif, M., *et al. Intergroup conflict and cooperation: the Robbers Cave experiment.* Norman, Okla.: Univ. of Okla. Press, 1961.

Shrieke, B. *Alien Americans.* New York: Viking, 1936.

Shuey, A. M. *The testing of Negro intelligence.* Lynchburg, Va.: J. P. Bell Co., 1958.

Snow, E. How it looks to Ivan Ivanovitch. *Sat. Eve. Post*, 1947, *219*, 23–25.

Sodhi, K. S., and Bergius, R. *Nationale Vorurteile; eine sozialpsychologische Untersuchung an 881 Personen.* Berlin: Duncker und Humblot, 1953.

Stagner, R. Studies in aggressive social attitudes. *J. soc. Psychol.*, 1944, *20*, 109–120, 129–140.

———— War and peace. In *Encyclopaedia of psychology.* P. L. Harriman (ed.)., 1946, 891–897.

Stoetzel, J. *Without the chrysanthemum and the sword.* London: Heinemann, 1955.

Stouffer, S. A., *et al. The American soldier.* Vol. 1. Princeton, N.J.: Princeton Univ. Press, 1949.

Strachey, A. *The unconscious motives of war.* New York: International Universities Press, 1957.

Torre, M. *Health and diplomacy.* Unpublished manuscript, 1962.

———— (ed.). *The selection of personnel for international service.* New York: World Federation for Mental Health, 1963.

UNESCO. Evaluation techniques. *Int. soc. sci. Bull.*, 1955, *7.*

Van Loon, F. H. G. Amok and lattah. *J. abnorm. soc. Psychol.*, 1927, *21*, 434–444.

Wallas, G. *Human nature in politics.* London: Constable, 1908; 3rd ed., 1929.

Walworth, A. *School histories at war.* Cambridge, Mass.: Harvard Univ. Press, 1938.

White, R. K. Misconceptions in Soviet and American images. Paper presented at meeting of American Psychological Association, New York, N.Y., Sept. 4, 1961.

World Federation for Mental Health. *Cross-cultural studies in mental health.* K. Soddy, ed. London: Tavistock Publications, 1961.

―――― *Mental health and world citizenship.* 1948.

―――― *Mental health in international perspective.* 1961.

World Health Organization, *The mental health implications of the peaceful uses of atomic energy.* 1959.

Wright, Q. *A study of war.* Chicago: Univ. of Chicago Press, 1942.

Zavalloni, M. Unpublished Ph.D. dissertation. New York: Columbia University, 1960.

SUPPLEMENTARY REFERENCES

Boulding, K. E. *Conflict and defense: A general theory.* New York: Harper & Row, 1961.

Etzioni, A. *The hard way to peace.* New York: Collier Books, 1962.

Fromm, E. *May man prevail?* New York: Doubleday, 1962.

Guetzkow, H., *et al. The use of simulation for research and teaching in international relations.* Englewood Cliffs, N.J.: Prentice-Hall, 1961.

Keller, S. *Beyond the ruling class.* New York: Random House, 1963.

Melman, S. *The peace race.* New York: Braziller, 1962.

Rapoport, A. *Fights, games and debates.* Ann Arbor: Univ. of Michigan Press, 1960.

Richardson, L. F. *Statistics of deadly quarrels.* Pittsburgh: Boxwood Press, 1960.

Singer, J. D. *Deterrence, arms control and disarmament.* Columbus: Ohio State Univ. Press, 1962.

INDEX OF NAMES

INDEX OF
SUBJECTS